IN A MIRROR

IN A MIRROR

REFLECTIONS FROM THE LIFE OF
JESUS CHRIST

RAED MIKHAEL

RESOURCE *Publications* • Eugene, Oregon

IN A MIRROR
Reflections from the life of Jesus Christ

Resource Publications
An Imprint of Wipf and Stock Publishers
199 W. 8th Ave., Suite 3
Eugene, OR 97401

www.wipfandstock.com

PAPERBACK ISBN: 978-1-5326-5520-3
HARDCOVER ISBN: 978-1-5326-5521-0
EBOOK ISBN: 978-1-5326-5522-7

Manufactured in the U.S.A.   09/28/18

In A Mirror

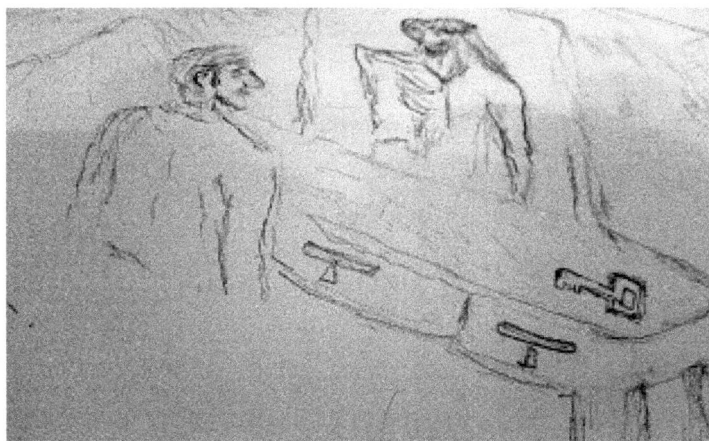

Table of Contents

Prologue

BLESSED IS THE LORD Jesus Christ, the source of all blessings and inspirations and the central character of my writing. I pray that the Lord may use the words of this book to bring perspective to its readers, changing lives where needed.

In A Mirror is a collection of essays on Christian terms which have lent themselves to many disciplines of philosophy and religion: destiny, desire, power, truth, faith, joy and righteousness, terms often watered down by frequent or abstract usage that take away from their original and intended meaning outside of the context of the word of God. The book's objective is to present an introductory discussion that would help define the meaning of these selected concepts using the bible as the only reference, giving evidence of its sufficiency as the infallible word of God, for all teaching, edification, and correction[1].

A testimony written after decades of isolation, the book is inspired by the life of an individual whose introspection lacked Christ, before he was shocked by the image of a man whom he does not recognize. Swaying back and forth, by all kinds of doctrines, beliefs and traditions in which negligence to the presence of God distanced the world from a purpose to life, I waited thirty years before a close-up encounter with Christ. Prior years I have maneuvered my affair with a considerable distance from Christ, keeping separate my spiritual development while attesting to questionable paths bordering atheism. Many times I have disregarded life with a slight irreverence to the fleeting sense of time and the normalized

---

1. 2 Timothy 3:16

1

imminence of death following years of aimless strife to survival. I contained my faith to the coping mechanisms in which reliance on human power dominated reason, resolving to my own strength to amend meaning to incomprehensible traditions. Disguised under traditions of growing up in a Christian family, I achieved a reasonable balance of faith in which I tailored God around my needs. While I retired my atheist's pursuits by a more moderate agnosticism, lacking the Holy Spirit, a relationship with Christ was void of the elements needed for conviction. It was the late experiences of the Holy Spirit that brought forth the testimonies in this book, which attest to the powerful work of God through Jesus Christ to reach individuals like myself.

Revealing, truths by the Spirit of God is like standing before a mirror for the first time. Shocking, I am certain, such an experience would most likely require a renewed avowal to self-rediscovery resulting from the new awareness of the self, realizing God's perspective has far deeper insights to life than the image we see of our own, putting to shame any efforts of achievements by the more likely dependence on the world. Limited to our own capacities, it is no surprise our lives away from Jesus Christ are reduced to a mere amalgamation of survival techniques which attempt to conjure an image about the self without introspection. Consequently, I find the exposition and experience of the Holy Spirit through God's revelation to be more of a conviction preceding a cognizant, logical, adoption of perceived values, of which merits are not lacking in the example of Jesus Christ. I, therefore, did not pursue a proof of the divinity of Jesus Christ as the One True God, the human representation of the Father, the Son, and the Holy Spirit, although it is my utmost desire for such truth to embolden its features from the haze of misleading doctrines in the present day. On the contrary, I considered the trinity to be the priori truth of my writings, on which my readers have knowledge, regardless of their belief system; or perhaps, they're destined by a similar calling of the word of God, ordained to salvation since the beginning of time[2],

2. Ephesians 1:4–5

to whom Christ revealed the mystery of salvation with an undeniable conviction.

Growing up as a son of a Seventh Day Adventist minister, I spent the early years of my childhood building strong attachments and fond memories of stories about God. My views of God were as varied as the denominations that represented Him, disconcerting by the numbers and variability of faiths. Further aggravated by my limited knowledge about the unity of God, it was consequential for my faith to partition my beliefs to a collection of ordinances disjointed in their agreement to my relationship with God, most evident of which was the dogmatic keeping of the fourth commandment regarding the Sabbath[3], which strongly posed contradictory views when held next to Sunday's worship services common in most other Christian churches. While the core principle values learned at Sabbath School were of no significant difference from other Christians, worship-day discrepancies mainly served to stray many away from the message of Christ centered on the love of God and those of our neighbors[4]. Comforting assurance always abounded in my frequent visits to neighboring churches of Catholic and Orthodox faiths where a greater fellowship with Christians overlooked any doctrinal differences with God, before complications of adulthood brought on a new meaning to rising denominational dissensions as the new norm that would cause many to ease away their faith in God.

Doing the work of missionaries, my family uprooted from many towns where they were assigned to build churches, which made it difficult to establish any strong attachment to one particular place, aside from a hopeful sense of strengthening God's outreach by unbounded measures—a "Christianity-Without-Borders"—a reality that would prove a lot more complex as spiritual sectarianism spread to the global phenomena we now live in. By relativity of faith, a greater freedom to exploration became a viable alternative to the more orthodox religions, giving way to

3. Exodus 20:8–11
4. Luke 10:27

a more convenient ideology by which a trend of a new world order emerged—a peaceful common humanity—which unified the
world with godless tenets against the disregard of man, based on
the most critical aspects of human identity, those related to origin,
religion, faith, color, creed, etc., leaving only acts of labor to entitle
them to an immutable birth right by virtue of being human. No
greater constituents were more amicable than those of such an
order, drawing many by its sacraments of free-will in spite of its
marked dogmatic challenges which it continues to dismantle by
unethical practices of an immoral system, replacing Christ from
the center by a similar faith in the power of the collective-self—the
safety in numbers—relaying on promises of a social order when
Christ's adoption is the only sacrificial sacrament required to eternal salvation. Inherent of western mythology and philosophy, a
new world order had spawned multiple of deities which appeal to
adherence by the common sense, that which parallels the diversity
of human thoughts in spite of the evidence to our systemically unified paths through cycles of life and death. While, on the other
hand, absolute truth presents decisive facts determine the way we
live and die, less concerned with homogenous peaceable unity if
rooted in lies that entirely undermine the most critical Christian
pillar, Jesus Christ. Spoken by Christ and the apostles, the word of
God is a "sword" of a decisive truth, given for a choice between two
paths, one leading to life in Jesus Christ and another to death, as
stated in the book of Matthew 10:34: *"Do not suppose that I have
come to bring peace to the earth; I have not come to bring peace, but
a sword."*; Ephesians 6:17 *"the helmet of salvation and the sword of
the spirit, which the word of God."*; Hebrews 4:12 *"For the word of
God is living and powerful, and sharper than any two-edged sword,
piercing even to the division of soul and spirit, and of joints and
marrow, and is a discerner of the thoughts and intents of the heart."*

Much remains to unfold by the divisiveness of the word of
God mentioned in the bible, most notably Christ's return which
will mark the fulfillment of history mentioned in the prophecies of Isaiah, Jeremiah, Ezekiel, Daniel, and finally the book of
Revelations—most touted historically for its mark of the beast

presented by the number 666: "*Here is wisdom, let him who has understanding calculate the number of the beast, for the number is that of a man; and his number is six hundred and sixty-six*" *(Revelation 13:18).* Many interpretations and predications have surfaced throughout history by which it's believed "666" will be among the last signs that beckons the return of Christ. This number I have seen recurrently in my life by no human coincide, through personal associations and relationship that recalled early memories of my Christian education and transpired my return to Christ. Nevertheless, I leave the more speculative prophecies to the tests of time. I believe it is far more important to hone in on the more critical aspects of Christianity, most importantly Christ, and His impertinence to salvation. I have, therefore, been made to believe that God goes through extraordinary measures to reveal Himself to those whom He calls. My testimony speaks to this truth, having redefined my understanding of Him as Savior—not only as a God—through personal experiences, where God's hands was unmistakably present. Surpassing boundaries and limitations of manmade religions and rituals, a life in Christ is a transition by the Holy Spirit from the mere acts of being Christian to a very close personal relationship with Christ. Christ overshadows our lives on earth, giving tremendous clarity and perspective, distinguishing between right and wrong, with strides in personal revelations that change our core values from the world's to those of Christs. Moreover, Jesus' life revealed God's divine secret ordained before creation, to reverse our aimless wandering by a more purposeful destination to heaven. A necessary change from the Christian status quo, that of a minister's son, by a more complete Christ-like life, in which we are called God's children. As David the psalmist most poetically wrote: "*But to all who did receive Him, to those who believed in His name, He gave the right to become children of God*" *(John 1:12).*

In *A Mirror* is a simple attempt at complex topics to those already familiar with Christ, reaffirming their stance on the more loosely defined terminologies that evade common spiritual beliefs. My hope is that this book will reinvigorate your questions about the purpose of your faith and your relationship with Jesus Christ, bringing about a favorable change to your life and others around you, replacing the lukewarm indifference characteristic of Christian dilettantes, by a more cognitive and causative desire to attain assurance to eternal life with Christ. I pray my writing encourages others to take a deeper look into Jesus Christ and share their testimony. Witnesses to the crucifixion and resurrection of Christ are the source of faith which has greatly impacted the world, making Jesus Christ among the most popularly published and influential figures in today's history.

I. Creation

> *Inadequate, photography of faraway galaxies takes us back to evolution theory's most egregious gap in its answer to our origin question.*

SPACE PHOTOGRAPHY IS ONE of the more promising man-made creations that have accelerated our understanding of the universe and the world around us, bringing to focus incredible depiction of the universe with stunning shots of earth's magnificent solar system relative to those of other planets and stars in the milky-way; albeit, inadequate, photography of faraway galaxies takes us back to evolution theory's most egregious gap in its answer to our origin questions by evasive theories that are inconclusive with regards to the initial matter that brought the world into order. In the vastness of the universe and the precise interdependencies that make up our most intricate creations on earth, the imprints of an impeccable designer are present everywhere, requiring a more perceptive mind over a less primitive creation to subdue and make meaning of its purpose. Living organisms allow for a greater understanding of our capacities as intelligent beings able to give and derive meaning from life, distinguishing differences between ourselves others, creating a hierarchal order of power through which we comprise our theories about God and life. Given words and language we are able to speak and understand, formulating ideas about who we are in relationship to the universe, and a much greater creator, by whom we must have been created for a reason, and whose power far exceeds that of creation. Seen at the microscopic levels and scaled to galaxy expansions, are efforts leading the investigation of the causative agents behind their perfect coherence, inspiring a figurative conversation with God and man, perhaps a modern Job, whose apprehensions about life's toils awakens the perceptive mind of a poetic Godly response: "*Where were you when I laid the earth's foundation? Tell me, if you understand. Who marked off its dimension? Surely you know! Who stretched a measuring line across it? On what were its footings set, or who laid its cornerstone—while the morning stars sang together and all the angels shouted for joy?*" (*Job 38:41*)

Bounded by incomplete theories of evolution[5], or the initial spark that brought the precise order of the universe into place, probabilistic theories[6] comprised no unified answers about the basic elements and their origin. Made of similar matter to those of plants and animals we find evidence of our human superiority mostly in the distinguishing consciousness that sets us apart from the acts of our closest genetic species. While presumptuous evolutionary theories far fetch the magnitude of time required to project in both past and future, it leaves doubt in the balance to a man impatiently fidgeting for an answer to life's purpose. A simple, self-evident presence of a higher God, who ordered the universe into being was made more complex by a man attempting to reason its own God-like superiority over others. Missing the mark on usability, mankind's upcycle of the truth: "*In the beginning God created the heavens and the earth. Now the earth was formless and empty, darkness was over the surface of the deep, and the Spirit of God was hovering over the waters*" (*Genesis 1:1,2*) reached unprecedented heights of defiance by evolutionary theories,

5. Pierre, Jean–Claude; La Lamarck, Antoine de Monet; The Origins of Species: 150th Anniversary edition, by Charles Darwin; Zoological Philosophy: An exposition with regards to the natural history of animals

6. Seif, Charles, Zero: The Biography of a Dangerous Idea

which falter by inconsistent proofs regarding the onslaught and self-governance of the precise laws of nature. Highly improbable, hypothesis of self-organizing blueprint of life's DNA lies in the domain of the impossible, unfounded by a short historic collective memory of humanity without any consistent proof. With certainty comparable to a random chance, self-evolution is similar to un-aided attempts of reverting colors of a painting to comprehensible uniformity from chaos, an example of which is in Figure 1, where mixed colors are reconfigured on their own into their individual color spectrum without any intervention. Similarly, big bang's ini-tial molecule couldn't have sparked life into the universe without the work of an agent, to bring viable order from absolute chaos.

> *The word of God is the power by which we establish truth about creation. Immutable, it is the sword by which a clear divide is made between darkness and light*

An egregious oversight to the calculations of our discoveries is discrediting God of creation, by similar inadequacy to excluding invisible light rays from the spectrum of light in spite of their felt evidence. In denial of an omnipotent creator, we are threatened by the existence of God whom we associate with the limiting agents of law and sin and whom we fear would spoil our self-exploratory inquisitions to much promised lead to controls when our con-sciousness is distant from Him. Equally disturbing is the exclusion, emphasized by invisibility, of evidence pointing to the existence of a supreme God. Powerful are the witnesses of God's creation seen in the interwoven preset conditions and mechanisms without which our entire humanity would spin to an unalterable disarray, escaping the harder question about our existence and its purpose. Evidenced by the basic elements with which we breathe, to the preciseness of the angular bonding between hydrogen and oxygen molecules in life-giving water, the earth's placement in relationship to the sun, and the constant laws that ground our physical bodies in gravity with an unlimited outlook into galaxies in a never-ending universe, expanding at an ever-accelerating rate. God's world is meticulously made.

I. Creation

Chaos

Order

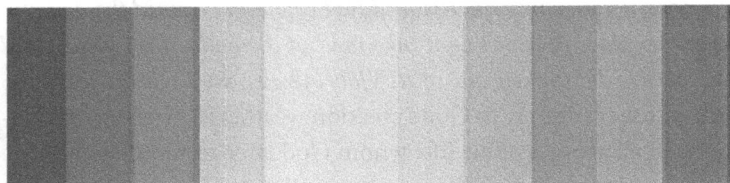

God who is capable of putting the world together in six days by His word, is also able to establish the proof of His work, most notable in the birth of His Son Jesus Christ whom He sent in human form, and sacrificed on the cross, so that His resurrection maybe witnessed by many who would become the living proof of His creation. A testament to Jesus' life remains to be the most viable evidence of the story of creation. By God's appearance in the flesh, Jesus has been given the authority of our destinies, promising a similar spiritual creation of us that is more reflective of His image. God's aspiration for perfect beings had to do away with the more mechanical aspect of earthly decaying humans, by a more complete being in which the constraint of death seen in the regrettable design of Adam and Eve in the story of creation is abolished by the resurrection of Christ from death. The invincibility to death presented in Jesus Christ extended to our lives as spiritual beings, worn by those whom would later adopt Jesus as their God—who catachrestically speaking— *"bear the groans of a new liberty into eternal life in heaven." (Romans 8:20),* the promise of an even greater creation from that in which we now experience.

Before we subdued our climates to escape the late serotinals for an early greenhouse harvest, the universe continues to operate in due seasons. The apple tree will always yield its fruit in the winter, by the same cycles in which its parent tree grew, relying on water, air, and sun to branch the luscious flowers that birds, bees, and animals feed on. The primeval will always bring the rain where rivers run and trees blossom. A greater truth emerges from the budding of the apple tree, the burial of the seed, more symbolic of the meaning about our life and death enters into our consciousness. A much higher wisdom of a creator must be attributed to God, who has commanded life from an inert seed: *"Have you commanded the morning since your days began, and caused the dawn to know its place, that it might take hold of the ends of the earth, and the wicked be shaken out of it?" Job (38:12),* were God's words to Job whose testimony to God's creation weathered grievous tribulations in all aspects of his life, whom God later restored by faith.

It may be worthwhile to consider the words behind the great designer of the universe, who took a far greater interest in our humanity than in any other creation. God has greater plan for our future, requiring belief in more than the fictitious façade we now chase in toiles and labors away from His truth, often mounting to nothing more than a psychological insignificance of passing vanities. Untamed timely pursuits to answers about life impacts our individual lives the most, when not aided by God's guidance and words, risking costly retreats to what has long been established about His creation

II. Life: A Poem

*"For You have delivered my soul from death, have you not
kept my feet from falling, that I may walk before God
in the light of the living?"*
(Psalms 56:13)

> *To the miracle of resurrection of Jesus Christ,
> in which light-giving life was not dwindled by
> death.*

I RECALL MANY EXPERIENCES in life that have made lasting and powerful impressions on me: being caught in a powerful blizzard of rain or snow with a sense of helplessness to the forces of nature; feeling the warm exuberance of the slowly ascending ball of fire during sunrise on top of a high mountain while watching the amazing sun rise in the distance. Such experiences bring much sense to our lives by the awe it instills to our perception of the greater universe that surrounds us. A much similar awe is felt by the Holy Spirit when praying to Jesus that all things in life fade to the background with whom encounters changes lives forever: *"But we all beholding the glory of the Lord with open face, are transformed into the same image from glory to glory, as by the Spirit of the Lord." (2 Corinthians 3:18)*.

I dedicate this poem about life to His Majesty, Jesus Christ, whom I owe my life to. *"For we didn't cunningly devise fables when we made known to you the power and coming of our Lord Jesus Christ, but were eye witnesses of His Holy Majesty." (2 Peter 1:16)*.

In a Mirror

Through life's joys and maladies,
In times of hope and times of uncertainty,
Through trials and tribulations in incomprehensible tragedies,
In cowardly control and invisible forces of evil capacity,

By winning and losing in illusory moments of arriving,
For continuous strife to sensational exaggeration and ambivalent dismay,
By strengths and weaknesses of things achieved and others depriving,
For contempt and in fulfillment, through fleeting perishables and lasting decay,

As powerful gentleness and weak violence,
To a life-giving breath in tightly interwoven creations,
As scathing scorn and praise leading to an immutable silence,
To the blue print of self-organizing molecules living to cessation,

In the mystery of human consciousness with its pursuit of survival,
Through uninterruptible cycles gravitating a tirelessly rotating earth,
By the law of death to a life-giving seed and life-fostering tree revival,
To the miracle of Jesus Christ, in which life was not dwindled by death.

III. Destiny

*"Blessed be the God and Father of our Lord Jesus Christ,
who has blessed us with every blessing in the heavenly
places in Christ, just as He chose us in Him before the
foundation of the world, that we should be holy and
without blame in Him, in love, having predestined us to
adoption as sons by Jesus Christ to Himself, according to
the good pleasure of His will."*
(Ephesians 1:3-5)

> *For no one knows – even those who claim Christ
> as the personal savior—their final destination*

I WAS PREDESTINED TO my family, like many, I had no choice to
my origin, faith, or stature. I am predestined to tomorrow, with
alterable choices that help augment life to a better living, by faith,
I believe it will change my path to the destiny which I desire, that
which I have no knowledge of, to a timely predestined death, of
which I have hopes of overcoming in Jesus Christ. We are predestined to heaven, with hopeful certainty, by faith in Jesus Christ;
for no one knows—even those who claim Christ as their personal
savior—their final destination; a posteriori fact to our priori short
sightedness into the future. Greater evidence of our predestination
is in Jesus' ordination of children to higher placement in heaven,
infants with no cognizant choice to salvation, *"At that time the
disciples came to Jesus and asked "who, then, is the greatest in the
kingdom of heaven?" He called a little child to him, and placed the*

child among them. And he said: "Truly I tell you, unless you change and become like little children you will never enter the kingdom of heaven. Therefore, whoever takes the lowly position of this child is the greatest in the kingdom of heaven. And whoever welcomes one such child in my name welcomes me." (Matthew 18:1 – 5). Those without a choice, whose breaths of life is justified outside our convoluted perception of knowledge or faith, children are destined by a higher regard in heaven than adults. Less concerned children are with complex knowledge about the kingdom of God, than adults striving for assurance to a destiny in Christ, who are called to a life of a balancing act of faith, at times contrary to popular ideology, to inherit the kingdom.

Lest we become boastful[7] of our salvation, or slack with confidence, God's contingency to the "fullness of time"[8] determines our faith's worthiness to heaven: *"for by grace you have been saved through faith, and that not of yourselves; it is the gift of God, not of works, lest anyone should boast. For we are His workmanship created in Christ Jesus for good works, which God prepared beforehand that we should walk in them." (Ephesians 2:8-10).* Hence, our predestination is known to an omniscience God, who has preset the future outside of time. More readily believed by a child who is less occupied with tomorrow, destiny is more complex to those with deeper grasp of the now, perplexed by the possibilities we have no control over. Tossing aside all events and preset conditions that caused us to arrive at the now—our origin, environment, faith, religion, etc.—or other unknowns to the entity of God. We live with a multiplicity of understandings about ourselves: some by an exuberance and awe to knowledge and wisdom, others by a fatalist pessimism and existentialist rigor, and some by a lukewarm indifference to the purpose and unpredictability of life. It is difficult to believe that the choices of our will, that which is evidenced by our chosen actions, has been preset with a driver in which our faith in an entity of God is its center, unless we consider all choices to have

7. 2 Timothy 3:2
8. Galatians 4:4–7

been preset before they happen: "*Truly, Truly, I say to you, before Abraham was I Am.*" *(John 8:58),* was Jesus report to His disciples, reflective of His knowledge of their destinies and His omnipresence across the dimension of time, of which they only had limited visibility of the now. Otherwise, it is difficult to believe that we had a choice to all the preset conditions of our lives to which we were born into, against or for which, we are given limited choices, before the predestined end that awaits us all in death. Without complete knowledge of the beginning and the end, our choices are guesses at best, based on past knowledge that may be made obsolete by an unknown tomorrow, to which we have been predestined. By faith of salvation in Christ we accept our lives' destiny, hoping that the unfolding of time does not reveal a different destination, concealed under a temporary illusion of our free-will choice, erring on perception, it had not been already known and predestined by God. Therefore, the learning of our fate would serve an incomprehensible blow to life for those with no assurance to salvation; for If I learned of my final damnation, why would I choose to live? Yet, how else might our faith be tested if not through the presumable unseen?

> *. . . our choices are guesses at best, based on knowledge that may be obsolete by an unknown tomorrow, to which we have been predestined.*

The incorporation of the most critical uncertainty in our consciousness, that which destines us to life, finds resemblance to that of our relationship with God; where one seeks affirmation in the establishment of the seen, the other is a result of the magnitude of our faith, in which the existence of God is confined to our limited knowledge of the unseen destiny. Apart from divine hope, most bothersome is the concept of predestination to the "free will" of man. Its acceptance revolts a feeling of helplessness to the reality of the now as a final destination; that which is passed is done away with, that which is to come we do not know. With preeminence of death aside, most detestable to our willful palate is predestination, requiring a rigorous dissipation of life's indifferences through a self-projected acquisition of things which vainly secure our grasp into the future, not the least of which is the imperfect and incomplete acquisition of works, in which we drive direction to a unified common understanding of the self, as a means to salvation. As a result, our "raison d'etre" changes from the absolute confidence of tomorrow to the historical guild of the now, shifting the strife from the unknown territory of the future, requiring a necessary act of faith, whose ethos are of a secondary hopeful significance, from a multitude of other dimensions and significances. Such a reliance on an imperfect knowledge of time orders our choices, giving precedence to things seen over those which we cannot see. We, in an act of empowered, collective, self-imposed ignorance, determine the exclusion of these things we cannot see: "*What must I do to inherit eternal life?*" asked the rich young ruler to Jesus, "*Sell all you have and distribute to the poor, and you will have treasure in heaven; and come, follow Me*" (*Luke 18:19-23*) was Jesus' response when the ruler left him to attend to the more tangible riches he had, which he valued over the unseen "*eternal life*". Hidden from us is knowledge of our destiny by the reality of the present, in which the adoption of an absolute act of faith forecasts a shadow of doubt on the premise that justifies a free gift of "salvation", difficult to reconcile with our consciousness on account of the multiplicities we live by.

Inspired by the Holy Spirit, our acts of faith align to God's will when we begin through the revelation of Christ to understand the grace by which God empowered meaning to our destinies; where we were once dead in time, we are resurrected with Jesus Christ outside of time, before we ever existed, when God made the world by His word: "*In the beginning was the Word, and the Word was with God, and the Word was God. He was in the beginning with God. All things were made through Him, and without Him nothing was made that was made. In Him was life, and the life was the light of men. And the light shines in the darkness, and the darkness did not comprehend it.*" (*John 1:1-5*).

III. DESTINY

> *justifying the interim time of life to chance*
> *. . . the will to choice must overlook all things*
> *unanswerable.*

Jesus Christ gave precedence to faith, to accept as our destiny to life, with greater openness to the possibilities outside our current limitation of this world, to the greater capacities of God and His power to accomplish above our expectations in this life, and by faith, in the resurrection which He predestined to us after, in heaven. Alleviated from our responsibility is the knowledge of our future destiny, or those of others, which had been given under Jesus' full authority and pre-knowledge before the beginning of time. Hence, our learned and inspired understanding changes the purpose by which we live to the fellowship with our source of life found in Jesus Christ, away from the concerns about the things of this world, hopeful to reach God's kingdom as our final destination. How else might we begin to interpret the purpose of life apart from that which had conceived us, or that which has destined us away? If not defined by its beginnings or its ends, the directional driven destiny does not exist, placing all its bets on the now, justifying the interim time of life to chance, in which the will to choice must overlook all things unanswerable.

Assuming the role of God in predicting destiny would be an act of hypocrisy done with futile estimations at best *"For many who were first will be last, and last will be first (Mark 10)"*, overlooking the purpose of our own destiny, confusing Jesus' hopeful assurance of salvation on unfounded interpretation of the word of God with borrowed reflection from the destinies of others. By such a limitation we operate, some by an inspired hopeful faith, others in maximizing exuberance of strife to the commodity of time, to unfolding events, purposing life on the relative pillars of a greater good. To some, destiny cannot simply converge to the path of God's son Jesus Christ—even if a one-dimensional established path to the complex multiplicities of an omnipotence being of God appears as the most obvious choice—when its trotting appears risky to an explorative ego that wishes to take its destiny into its will, distancing itself from the uncertainty of tomorrow, betting on an incomplete grasp of the unseen. Albeit, there lies our greatest aspirations to progress in life; not in the things passed, or the realm of the now, but in the light and faith of the things to be, to those whom God saved in Jesus Christ, *"Who are born, not of blood, nor of the will of the flesh, nor of the will of man, but of God."* *(John 1:13).*

God's eternal destiny predates time, with our lives' events unfolding as a testament to the strength of our faith in the words and life of Jesus Christ is the promise of our final destiny and salvation. However, strangely these aspirations may have steered us down the wrong paths to discovery, predestined, the reworking of our faiths can be distraught in costly discouragement to our progress. The answer is easily challenged to a faith in an abstract destiny of salvation where in the nuance simplicity of mere breath of existence, lies all the permutations of life of eternal mortals in Jesus Christ's resurrection. For our marked finale has been claimed to its viewers before its beginning through Jesus Christ, leaving a continuing series to an act of faith of our free will.

IV. Desire

> *No more has desire to freedom been more val-
> ued in the sight of God than when He demon-
> strated His plans to free man from the slavery
> to the law by the life-giving sacrifice of Christ
> . . .*

I HESITATED BETWEEN LOVE and desire before writing this reflection, for they are often tied together, more times than not, con-
fused with one another. I thankfully remembered 1 Corinthians
chapter thirteen, when I resolved to defer my beliefs about love
to that chapter, which is more anointed with my new definition
of love achieved through the perfection of Jesus Christ. A close
relative of love is desire; its biblical origin in Genesis (3:6) *"so when
the woman saw that the tree was good for food, that it was pleasant
to the eyes, and a tree desirable to make one wiser, she took of its
fruit and ate. She also gave to her husband with her, and he ate."*
Eve's desires were misguided by the serpent that lead her to eat
from the forbidden tree of knowledge, becoming the bible's anchor
story by which the message of salvation develops at great length,
through historical kingdoms, extending to spiritual domains that
have flourished on its basic principle of good versus evil. Created

with desires, God has given Adam and Eve the wisdom to choose without knowing the difference between good and bad, and one clear explicit instruction: "to not eat from the tree of knowledge." With much disharmony as by a willful desire of dissonant instrument, deviating from a rehearsed orchestral score, Eve's oversight to eat of the forbidden tree must have had a debilitating and embarrassing effect to God's ears, the conductor of their lives. God's subsequent encounter with Adam and Eve must have been awkward given their new awareness of their nakedness before God, who now must reconsider His orchestral score of creation in a hotly debated series of "whose fault is it?!" between an omnipotent God and His free-willed creation defying His sovereignty, seeking expulsion from Eden on account of desirable exploration of the forbidden.

Spawning many ethical disciplines of law pertaining to civil liberties and human rights, to the free-will of man attaining his rightful place to life by choice, no more has desire to freedom been valued in the sight of God than when He demonstrated His plans to free man from the slavery to law by the life-giving sacrifice of Christ, who would reverse the defiance entered by Adam to mankind. Such remediation, arising from man's imperfections and difficulty to differentiate between good and bad desires, is often times misguided by the non-spiritual nature of earthly flesh, to which Adam and Eve more readily yielded, succumbing to its gravitational pull of death. By enticement to future slavery, the "serpent" leveraged the much covetous desires to knowledge with which Eve would break an explicit commandment given by God: *"But the fruit of the tree which is in the midst of the garden, God said "You shall not eat of it, nor shall you touch it, lest you die.""* (*Genesis 3:6*). Prior, perhaps God watched Adam and Eve from a distance as they rehearsed, slaughtered, skinned and devoured, shuffling hastily between racks of food, unknowingly indulging in all sorts of pleasures, perfecting their instrumental desires to discovery. The scores of their meals decimated and scattered, before they entered into the clearly marked forbidden zone, to entertain an internal lustful debate that would expose a desire they would rather have lived without: knowledge. When God breaks the silence of the noticeable awkwardness of their shuffled space, Adam and Eve's lack of preparedness to answer Him is exposed by their attempt to speedily recover their act, and muzzle God's company, sparingly welcoming His approach as with a delightful expectancy. God's mannered entrance, diminished through hesitation and interruption to their new acute instinctual reality, doubted its need to unfold. They turned towards Him as though composing a profound revelation, partly agitated by the discourse of their encounter. They murmured nervously as they fumbled through surrounding objects that would hide their new awareness, setting aside any traces of chopped "apples". They smile nervously to God's question about the tree, refocusing their rapid thoughts about His reproach in slowly passing minutes full of anxiety about the disparities between the sensory feast that belied them, and the disgust in the uncertainty of their companionship. Exhilarated by the euphoria of their new knowledge, their gaze roaming to mentally fetch another prey in the distance. God's dismissal is the first of a swarm of thoughts that would later disguise His absence from their new exploratory, limitless desires resolving Him to on-call duties. As God's warning divulged its appending intoxication into Adam and Eve's consciousness, they balanced between their new pursuits of desires and the justification for any ventures only for its mere enjoyment, at times egregious in their efforts of dissonance, others in exhilarated, self-fulfilling achievements.

> *. . . exhausting the balance between apathy and want that have collapsed the power of Samson by his desires to Delilah (Judges 16:19-30).*

Reiterated and expounded, covetousness impregnated more evil desires that characterized subsequent stories of the bible, shown in the murder of Abel by Cain to the necessary Godly eradication of humanity's idolatrous looting witnessed in Noah's age, and the ambitious naiveté of man in attempting to build the tower of Babel. It will soon follow that God's own people would engage in all sorts of idolatry and covetous acts that link back to the original sin. Made more appealing by the serpents advertising claims to man to become God-like, man easily fell to learn of his nakedness and shame, which he will have to train his entire life to the virtues of obedience to God's laws, right and wrong, when prior to their disobedience, such a refrain was not within their awareness or domain of responsibilities. It is therefore most true that *"When desire has conceived, it gives birth to sin; and sin, when it is full grown, brings forth death." James (1:15).*

The classic example of sin conceived by desires is a recurring theme to many of our lives today in our struggles between that which we can do to that which we must not, exhausting the balance between apathy and want that have collapsed the power of Samson by his desires to Delilah (Judges 16:19-30).

In our judgement of good and bad we are more keen to the laws of man in their appeal and applicability to our immediate senses, guided by others with similar desires of the flesh to our own *"For laying aside the commandment of God, you hold the tradition of men..." Mark (7:8).* God, often the victim of our dissipated attention to His invisibility, suffers from our defiance to His laws which we supersede by the earthlier man, toiling to leave a legacy, creating legacies of evasive icons, from which he can draw strength, fulfilling a much desirable need to ephemeral man-created senses, while escaping the more spiritual aspects of attaining the more perfect desires of God. Desire which God has demonstrated in His more perfect sacrifice to redemption of His children is marred by the more selfish gratification and boasting of the evil desires that entered man through knowledge, conceiving spirits of adultery, fornication, uncleanness, lewdness, and idolatry *(Galatians 5:19),* in place of the more valued aspiration to attain God's love and those of our neighbors.

IV. Desire

> *... we all pursued our desires, good and evil, as in a contest to witness which of the two would win, embarrassed mostly when faced with accountability to our superiors.*

Given time, we all pursued our desires, good and evil, as in a contest to witness which of the two would win, embarrassed mostly when faced with accountability to our superiors. We desire to be "like God", just as the serpent suggested to Adam and Eve that we're willing to reason ourselves over the will of others—most magnanimously God's—to attain that which we know to be undesirable. Lacking a Godly unifying virtue, our laws of desires are the most discordant disarray of judgements seeking mostly to devour that which is not ours. In the deeds of evil desires to which sin is born, we have all become guilty by the law, for by knowledge comes the repercussions of its application, where law is applied. Where we have gravid desires, we insufficiently held the law to our own judgment, requiring a blood sacrifice, a redemption of our mediator, Jesus Christ, who through the good will of God, died to fulfill God's desire of man's salvation. Instigated by His love for Adam and Eve, we would become heirs to the His everlasting kingdom, through Christ, having the desires to discernment of all that is good for edification and not for destructive desires: *"therefore I write these things being absent, lest being present I should use sharpness, according to the authority which the Lord has given me for edification and not for destruction." (2 Corinthian 13: 10).*

In our pursuits of righteousness, our freedom to desires are restored in the perfect love of Jesus.

V. Knowledge

"The fear of the Lord is the beginning of wisdom."
(Proverb 9:10)

KNOWLEDGE, IN WORDS, CARRY meaning that's associated with the totality of our experiences in time, where we have strong beliefs supported by evidence of truths, in all facets of life, ever evolving. Knowledge of God begins with His Word in which He reveals Himself to us, as it were before time began: *"In the beginning was the Word, and the Word was with God, and the Word was God. He was in the beginning with God. All things were made through Him, and without Him nothing was made that was made. In Him was life, and the life was the light of men. And the light shines in the darkness, and the darkness did not comprehend it." (John 1:1-5).* A result of the word of God is knowledge of ourselves, who we are, the knowledge of others, and the knowledge of things to which we have established learning about God in Jesus Christ. Knowledge is a discipline rooted in the fear of the Lord, the source of all knowledge, according to the word of God in Proverbs: *"The fear of the Lord is the beginning of knowledge, but fools despise wisdom and instruction." (Proverbs 1: 7).* In spite of any predisposition that may have contributed to my knowledge of Christ, like those by virtue of birth, or otherwise, heeding to: *"My son, hear the instructions of your father, and do not forsake the law of your mother." (Proverbs 1:8),* the knowledge of the Lord is complete by the revelation of something more than our mere cognitive senses, best described as God's Holy Spirit. Rooting the knowledge of words by experience, as birth is grasped through labor, so is the Holy Spirit's emergence from a renewed revelation of truth in Jesus Christ—that which does not require definition, but through revelations, becomes the totality of knowledge, through words and life.

> *"for wisdom is a defense as money is a defense, but the excellence of knowledge is that wisdom gives life to those who have it"* Ecclesiastes 7:12

While I have aspired and admired many theologians and thinkers of our times in their pursuit of knowledge, their central inquiry about the meaning of life I found to be best portrayed in the divine intervention established by God the Father through His Son Jesus on the cross, where I have discovered multidimensional literary and philosophical fulfillment sufficiently good to life. Most profoundly is the Christly reversal of social norms calling an eye-for-an-eye and tooth-for-a-tooth, prevalent during Moses' times, which Jesus replaced with higher morals of forgiveness, later perfected on the cross, as a remediation to our rebellious and wrathful sins. Surpassing knowledge, by His supernatural resurrection and ascension into heaven, Jesus promised a similar perfection for all God's children. Therefore, I have retired my understanding of the more worldly wisdom resulting from knowledge measured through power and wealth, to the more Christly values of the supernatural dimensions, in which I have rested my hopes on, those pertaining to the witnessed miracles performed by Jesus Christ, up to His resurrection and His subsequent gift bestowal of the Holy Spirit: *"for wisdom is a defense as money is a defense, but the excellence of knowledge is that wisdom gives life to those who have it"* Ecclesiastes 7:12. Inconclusive was my evidence to any prescribed path promising any fulfilling advancement to either, except through the path established by the revelation of Jesus Christ promising ultimate inheritance to eternal life. Hence my most reliant self-evident testimony: *"Trust in the Lord with all your heart, and lean not on your own understanding; In all your ways acknowledge Him, and He shall direct your path."* (Proverbs 4:2-6).

Such testimony defiles the random curiosity to knowledge originated by Adam and Eve by which God's prohibition to the tree of knowledge was overlooked, imparting all human acts and morals to the renewed covenant through Christ by His intermediary death to rectify man's sins. Evolved, sin morphed to a more complex model of power-centrism on which systems of trades developed modern day society, driven primarily by pursuit of wealth through knowledge, attached to our values, and in spite of their fleeting nature, portrayed in a plethora of recurring tragedies like those of Adam and Eve's. Job's example on the other hand, is the reversal of the rewards and punishment shown in the story of Adam and Eve, where there was no purpose to his incurred affliction outside the divine trial of a righteous man's attachment to wealth and their implication to his knowledge of God. A less elaborate trial is later given in the book of Mark, between Jesus and the law keeping rich man whose relationship to wealth, demonstrated a better view of the kingdom's precepts regarding earthly riches, and the narrow possibility it presented to access heaven. By similar knowledge, I have been a witness to many whose pursuit of knowledge to power and wealth, have been rewarding in exuberances of triumphs over the forces of humans and nature, while others' a complete and utter failure in warfare tragedies. For *"knowledge puffs up"*, as written in 1 Corinthians 8:1-3 *"but love edifies. And if anyone thinks he knows anything, he knows nothing yet as he ought to know. But if anyone loves God, this one is known by Him."* Hence, matching our random curiosity to knowledge and power is uncertain due to its betting on knowledge that is established outside the precepts of the knowledge of God.

> *"...matching our random curiosity to knowledge and power is the uncertainty by which we bet on knowledge that is established outside the precepts of the knowledge of God"*

Whether out of joyful divine interjection or out of fear, it may be pondered that the knowledge of God without an intermediary manifestation—knowledge uninspired by the Spirit of God—may lose its reverence to a mere ritualistic dogmas of moral obligations of a distant God. Closer was God's greatest achievement to reach His creation *"And without controversy great is the mystery of godliness: God was manifest in the flesh, justified in the Spirit, seen of angels, preached unto the Gentiles, believed on in the world, received up into glory." 1 Timothy 3:16,* abolishing the ritualistic laws and speculative beliefs of an unreachable God to the minds and hearts of humans. Many who have misapplied knowledge of the manifestation of Christ by unfounded mythological tales, hypothesizing through gnostic interpretation the dynamics of creation on which there is no coherent divine truth away from the incoherent fragments of Mesopotamian and Ancient Egyptians—an inscriptions of idols, in the shape of man-made carved images, or natural elements of the earth and the solar system—only served to establish more evidence of the existence of a spiritual domain that is outside of our physical world. While not implicitly stated in the word of God, the making of such idols and spirits have been explicitly forbidden by God for their useless inanimate nature and their defiance of His omnipotence, which Jesus' resurrection put an epic defeat to their myths. Although plausible for a more powerful creator to remorsefully, and perhaps incomprehensibly out of love, attempt to prevent His creation from the misery of sin leading to death, the mystery behind God's sacrificial love in Jesus Christ's death and resurrection, is a motive that may not be fully known or understood, *"For who has known the mind of the Lord that he may instruct Him? But we have the mind of Christ." (1 Corinthians 2:16).* Hence, the acknowledgement of a higher being, i.e. God, is the beginning of an incomplete path to establish knowledge in the face of uncertain existence to a mortal creation that struggles to derive meaning beyond the present tangible reality. Establishing a far simpler knowledge to life, Jesus' invitation to salvation is the child-like concept of cause-and-effect, where spirit inspired belief grants acknowledgment of God's choice of our salvation, we are effectually edified by faith to eternal life in heaven, for it is not constrained to the individual knowledge, but rather through the knowledge of the word of God: "*Therefore flight shall perish from the swift, the strong shall not strengthen his power, nor shall the mighty deliver himself.*" (Amos 2:4).

> *I find the purpose in which we exist to be vainly insufficient and incomplete without the exemplary love offered on the cross through Jesus Christ, giving life to those who believe in Him*

Finally, I find the purpose in which we exist to be vainly insufficient and incomplete without the exemplary love offered on the cross through Jesus Christ, giving life to those who believe in Him. I often question God's purpose to creation, which I find to be His strongest evidence to perfect knowledge: is there any rewarding fulfillment to an act of creation for an omniscience God? As the story of crucifixion strongly points to remediation by divine intervention, it parallels a glimpse into a creator's contemptuous doubt, where the obvious subjectivity in the reciprocal relationship between the creation and the creator is at risk. Burdened by imbalances in knowledge, the idolatrous godly character aspiration of God's closest image of His creation in man, are most dramatically played out in a trans-historic knowledge of impending cross-cultural apocalypse. Unrealized, end-times present immediate demands that decentralize a free-willed interdependency between God and egotistically curious man, where both strife for simultaneous control of a single-drive vehicle, quickly approaching a stop sign. Primed by a collective historical and archeological memory, and baffled by incomplete account of matters relating to knowledge of a creation impending death, I am consoled only by God's wisdom in revealing Himself to those whom He chooses, to the shrinking Solomon's of our age, who find wisdom to be quickly replaced by the more intolerable barbarians, in quest of control and power through an incomplete account of knowledge, void of any moral obligations, to realize *"that which has been is what will be, that which is done is what will be done, and there is nothing new under the sun." (Ecclesiastes 1:9).*

VI. Shame

"For idols speak delusion, the diviners envision lies, and tell false dreams; they comfort in vain. Therefore, the people wend their way like sheep; they are in trouble because there is no shepherd."
(Zechariah 10:2)

For she must have reasoned her folly to the pleasures of ignorance, the disregard for chastity in the pressing heat of incurring moments.

SHE LEARNED HER SHAME from her idol lovers' gaze; she knew her worth in their bosoms. Her aspirations in the contest of her peers, as if looking in a present day tabloid with sensational provocative displays of her glamorous body and bold headlines of look-alike models of comparable beauties. Her thoughts focused on her next encounters and the stories she will foretell all her friends; the souvenirs she'd won in spoils and splendor, now a wilted memory on her vanity mirror. She's beautiful since birth; that's all she knew. She never thought she would be caught in the quarrelsome mires of judgment when she desired something more than her lover's assuring fondles. For she must have reasoned her folly to the pleasures of ignorance, the disregard for chastity in the pressing heat of incurring moments. Void of reason, dignified by her rights to escape the moral judgments, she runs in search of her affairs that would soon seal her fate. In absence of judgment, her feet race to the fulfillment of her desires, never questioned, she would recount the glorious memories of her youth, when she sat amongst the riches of shame, behind the wealth of time that she had not befriended. Learning its vices by her crawls of leisure, readily dispensed to her revivals. Reassuring her glories, taken to the destitute of her unquenchable needs, the love affairs she squandered on the air of a sensation she had mistaken for love and self-worth. Her wisdom had left to those who pitied her. To the scorns of their idols that were paralyzed to the change of times, leaving scars on her face to be recognized by those who would later deny her feasts of their shame. Irreverent in the fact of things not attained, a lukewarm reality sets her to the past in search of the heated fervency that she once knew, only to find that it's been replaced by cold indifferences and judgment. She has to recover her nakedness in shadows of others whose light exposed her withering beauties, when a gentleness of a stranger would ensure her rescue, putting to rest the shame of those ready to stone her.

In the busy corners of town, courting the throngs of street crowds that gathered to scorn her, some knew her, while others, eagerly cheerful, edged to the moral grounds of their judgment, picking-up its mortar from the stones below their feet, slowly vengeful with an ascending temper. She was lusciously gullible, concealed behind a naïve veil with comparable passion to the eager desires of the crowds that she had once fornicated with. In loss for words and thoughts, she sought affirmation to her voluptuous beauty, which has, for long, supplied her with her sense of being as her only affirmation. Brought to his temple, He was virgin-like, an innocent observer, awkwardly out of place, and comfortable conforming to her essence as if familiar with her since time, separating her, if only for a moment's time, from all that's about her and in her. Her mind doubtful and anxious about His intentions and the conflict she was about to endure as a result of harbored shame under a sheltered vision of her love affairs' impending application of law, unfolding on a defamed harlot. She nervously and silently pleaded for a merciful moderator who would rescue her life from the gathering crowds before she caught a glance of a man who would secure her escape.

> *Woman, where are they? Has no one con-demned you?" She said, "No one, Lord." And Jesus said, "Neither do I condemn you; go, and sin no more. (Matthew 8:11)*

As such I imagine the story of the adulterous woman—symbolic of God's church—the bride and her first encounter with Jesus. A calumny of loveless, persecuted, compromised, corrupt, lifeless, gullibly believing, and lukewarm[9] woman. Jesus begins to reconcile her to herself, diverting the evils that were about to ensnare her shameful act, changing her destiny away from those who sought her life. In an act of humility, He draws on the commonality of those whose secret lives interlaced with her sins, kneeling to silently write on the ground the shame of those who concealed her arrest, calming away harassing roars of crowds, out-of-bound with their own rights, seeking to stone her. *But God chose the foolish things of the world to shame the wise; God chose the weak things of the world to shame the strong (1 Corinthians 1:27).* A reminder to remove the speck before the log, Jesus' glance at the wretchedness building up in her eyes, lit by the scorns of the ensuing crowds, clears the heaviness of those logging to stone her by the speck of a finger, on grounds of her shame. Her rights regained, she would pray for a second chance to life.

9. Revelations chapters 1 to 4; the seven churches of Ephesus, Smyrna, Pergamos, Thyatira, Sardis, and Laodicea's.

Gracefully determined, with strength of an iron fist, Jesus would promise to "dash to pieces" her fears. Thyatira of the crowds, the prostitute, whom the Lord likened to His church. She is to hold fast to her repentance, overcome her shame, learn the diligence of the saints, and await her Ephesus, Christ, her "first love". Without the allure of false lovers—the prophets of lies—she is to commit to memory the one whose love saved her from the compromising crowds, those like Pergamos, looking to devour her. Their fangs subdued, Jesus' steered their mouths away. Having been dead to compassion and mercy, the multitudes' appetites for preys was ferocious to their idolatrous Nicolaitan—the Balaam of destruction—the Sardis of death, seeking to kill by words and deeds, sacrificing all that befalls them. Raised from the spiritual death, Jesus words silences her accusers: *"Woman, where are they? Has no one condemned you?" She said, "No one, Lord." And Jesus said, "Neither do I condemn you; go, and sin no more." (Matthew 8:11).*

By hope she regains her life through Jesus who became the stone they were about to throw at her, held by His merciful judgement of their deeds, fulfilling the prophecy: *"Behold, I lay in Zion a stone of stumbling and a rock of offence: And he that believeth on him shall not be put to shame." (Romans 9:33).*

Like the bridegroom to His bride, so is God's desire for His church to place Him back in the center as the source of all perfect work. To remove the repulsive lukewarm, cheapened, and displaced love of the harlot's affairs, by which the truth of the church had been forsaken to a façade of traditions: *"Thus you nullify the word of God by the tradition you have handed down." (Mark 7:13).* For it is through Jesus and his restorative powers that we avert God's judgement from His repenting church, away from the shame of the idolatrous harlot and her fornication with foreign gods, for *"The wise shall inherit glory, but shame shall be the legacy of fools." Proverbs 3:35.*

VII. Sin

Those who have attempted to escape it, found sin's source in the unescapable self, inseparable from who we are, like the tares that grow with the crop...we choke and wilt to death.

SIN, THE BIRTH OF evil desires, the explicitness of *"the works of the flesh manifest, which are fornication, uncleanness, immodesty, luxury, idolatry, witchcraft, enmities, contentions, emulations, wraths, quarrels, dissensions, sects, envies, murders, drunkenness, revelry"* *(Galatians 5:19-21)* as well as, the more implicit, loosely defined acts of covetous desires, vanities, sloth, gluttony, greed, and various wicked acts, which when born, root back to the consciousness of the flesh induced by Adam and Eve, the source of all acts. To all compilation of acts to which wrongs have been ascribed, of the limitless moving boundary we call sin, against which a moral compass is often disregarded. Its marketing schemes have lavishly normalized the shades of sin, to blurry its boundaries into our psyche, evading "childish" ideals and beliefs about a better place from the world we live in, a permanent heaven away from the fleetingness of life in the present world. Archaic, sin's etymology has been

replaced with the more palatable immorality—the relative sin—
more comfortable with a system of recognitions and punishments,
shelfing the legacy of the term to a labyrinth convoluted theologies
and terminologies, the likes of which are: errors, faults, wrongs,
guilt, offenses and the like.

Those who have attempted to escape it, found sin's source in
the unescapable self, inseparable from who we are, like the tares
that grow with the crop, the polluted air of the oxygen we breathe,
adulterated, it causes us to choke and wilt to death. Efforts to de-
tract the good from the bad fails on one's own account, for who can
fight nature, or the urge to which we yield as detraction from that
which we desire, rarely distinguishing between the evasive sense of
right and wrong. The desire to the one remaining forbidden tree, in
place of the collection of all of the others yielding fruits, we freely
move the boundaries to avail the forbidden to the territory of the
allowed. As such was Eve's reasoning demonstrating the strange
frontier of sin; the breaking of covenant with God on account of an
inherent curiosity represented by a cunning serpent. Empowered
by Adam, its strength found grounds in cowardly unity that would
withdraw responsibility to cast the blame on Eve when questioned
before the ultimate authority of God. Bravery was never a righteous
quality in the face of authority, having to retreat deliberate acts of
desires to which premediated ignorance shoveled a path to unas-
sailable knowledge, in which treacherous battles would be ignited
with the self, for generations to come. Combatting that which we
cannot understand, the ineffective traditions masking the fron-
tiers of sin under the banner of knowledge—the attainment of the
forbidden fruit—to succumb a mortal soul to acceptance of sin
as a destiny to life, without a cure. Overlooking the promise and
the power that was gifted by Jesus Christ for sanctification and
redemption, sin has become integral to our beings, normalized by
the atrocities of our history.

> *Many partook in a sub-optimal decision to cru-
> cify the Son of God, forgoing any faint sense of
> reason to a mistrial of an innocent man.*

More comfortable we are in storing our oats to secure tomorrow; we value the bread over the "bread-of-life", we bubble over in an over-achiever mode to secure the little flour and oil that make our cake, while we eat it, too. Boiled, the frog hardly realized the rising temperature of the waters before it considered hopping to life, where it would be hardly blamed on account of its limited cognition. More elaborate, our brains can reason better than many frogs, ravens, or lilies, albeit; arrayed better than any of us, we still worry about what we eat and how we dress. Are we not worth much more than these? As a child I understood sin through the rituals I inherited from my guardians, the simple approvals of rewards and punishment to which I have established my ways to reconcile the differences in their worldly applications, by which agreement was seldom attained, if ever. I simply believed in the stories of crucifixion and the resurrection as the means to salvation, the escape from the lukewarm pot before it boils, and assurance to the everlasting life beyond the end of the world. Such make belief stories, I cherished without a shadow of doubt, much more strengthened by the testimonies of the word of God and the church, that reaching adulthood stupefied their simplicity by self-made contraptions of covetous, idolized and worshiped gods, who had no evidence or base in truth or in word.

Having falsely persecuted Jesus' to the cross, nowhere is the concept of sin better exhibited than in the evasive accusation of the Pharisees and Sadducees against Christ who challenged their authority and their theological doctrines, by which they felt the "rug being pulled from under their feet." By the release of Barnabas, they would, alternately, "brush under the rug" any evidence of the miracles they witnessed to "forgive sin", raise the dead, and heal the sick that have threatened their positions of power. Many partook in a sub-optimal decision to crucify the Son of God, forgoing any faint sense of reason to a mistrial of an innocent man. In unity, their sin has been diluted by a mediocre criminal whose release was more tolerable to content with than the prophetic changes they lived and witnessed by Jesus. Influenced by their normalizing act of will-to-power, Pilate would triage judgment to Herod, having found no fault in Jesus. The verdict points to a critical mistrial that would change the course of history to an egotistical majority and their leaders, seeking to get away with murder. Typical of offenders, they hardly account for all possible outcomes, when through Jesus' resurrection, they are dismayed by their own follies to believe the one who had come to deliver them from their sin. Giving rise to many followers, the promised Holy Spirit, would soon arrive on the few who had humbly accepted the simple truth that has manifested itself before their eyes.

Although not eradicated, much leverage from sin has been given by the arrival of the Holy Spirit on those who believe in the remedial sacrifice of Jesus Christ, in whom there was no sin. The invisible Helper whose indicative presence is not physical, but spiritual. Much like the abstraction of sin, the Holy Spirit would empower our choices against sin, to righteousness, that we may testify of the power of the Jesus and His cross. Our attempts to justification by our acts have otherwise failed repeatedly, that we've given up to timely death over a weak will of a short-lived life. Through time, God would allow our choices to trial by sins that have morphed into the idols of man's tradition, to determine our choice to faith, that in our righteousness we may do away with sin to become a representation of Jesus' body, suffering in a similar manner as He did, perhaps not only physically, but more drastically, spiritually, fighting against the inner being of sin—ourselves—the inexplicable call to lawlessness and evil desires that we have no means of dispensing apart from Christ: *"for our struggle is not against flesh and blood, but against the rulers, against the authorities, against the powers of this world's darkness, and against the spiritual forces of evil in heavenly realms." (Ephesians 6:12).* According to God's word, our struggles would justify our attainment to eternal life, as an alternative to our spiritual death, in which our pleasurable existence is the ephemeral debase away from Christ. And that's not by works, for the inspiration of change from sin, does not abolish sin, only the will to it: *"For we maintain that a man is justified by faith apart from the works of the law" (Romans 3:28).* We still have our rituals of worship by which we enslave the works of the flesh to the glory of God, as a means to derail us from our desires to sin. For we are the light of the world, the vessels of the Holy Spirit, created for good works preset by the Father before creation, have the burden of reconciling our understanding of the world to those of the teachings of Jesus Christ, less from a place of judgement, but through love in all things, following the example of Him who died for our sins.

Instead, at the center, we replace the Spirit of God by the anxious strife to a relentless acquisition of meaningless trophies which we've crowned to our self-worth. In recognitions and punishments, we acclimated to a more common system of norms, adjusting the moral compass of our consciousness by the approvals of others, allowing for greater complexities in accommodation of our differences as means of normalizing the range of human behavior, usually driven out of ruthless acts of incomprehensible wrath to power and recognition; the repeatable crucifixion of Christ in others by denial of their lives in our rightful convictions. Being victimized we seek to oppress, forgetting the immutable capacities of the oppressors, escalating our lives to unquenchable fires of hate immodestly demanding eradication. It is most challenging to "turn the other cheek" or forgive "seven times seventy" the trespasses of others, stowing away these morals to the more practical application of controls and manipulation of others. Pleasurably fornicating with desires, overlooking their brief façade in the short incline infinitely placed at a distance—never reachable—at a state of continuous strife without ever arriving. We created gods out of images, others envied to murder, finding unsustainable soothing calmness in luxurious drunkenness as meaningless alternative to quarrels and dissensions, *"For idols speak delusion, the diviners envision lies, and tell false dreams; they comfort in vain. Therefore, the people wend their way like sheep; they're in trouble because there is no shepherd/ (Zechariah 10:2).*

To all vanities yielding to the excessive attainment of self-gratification, in all perishable things attainable and conducive to the elevation of living, in knowledge of things that are and things to be, in greedy provisions to the self and others, through nakedness and fashionable attires, in random acts of kindness emanating from wicked motives, in fleeting moment of pleasure conceived to a depreciable memory, I rarely found a new sin under the sun. In return to my childhood, however; I always questioned: why are we here?

"*Come and let us return to the Lord, for He has torn, but He will heal us; He has stricken, but He will bind us up.*" *(Hosea 1:10-12)*

VIII. The Cross

*"Not by works of righteousness which we have done, but
according to His Mercy He saved us through the washing
of regeneration and renewing of the Holy Spirit, whom
He poured out on us abundantly through Jesus Christ our
Savior, that having been justified by His grace we should
become heirs according to the hope of eternal life."*
(Titus 3:5 – 7)

---

*Not always concealed, as in the case of Jesus'
crucifixion, our cross is usually the weight imparted to our life, hidden behind the veil of acts
steering our paths.*

DURING A 3-DIMENSIONAL MOVIE preview one hardly grasps the
full features of the movie without the special lens which modi-
fies our perception to the actual format of the displayed images on
the screen. Very similar to God's perception of us through Jesus
Christ, who became God's lens in the cross by which we became
a livelier multidimensional feature. Otherwise distorted by an incomplete dimension is the lens with which we see one another and
God. Perfection are always tainted by our own perceptions and
experiences. Much clearer an image is to whom is given the perfect lens—God—who sees in all dimensions of human character;
nothing is hidden from him. Being much stronger, God aided our
weaker pursuits to life by a much prevalence of His Son on the
cross and His Holy Spirit, that our weak peripheral vision gained

much light in preview of God's strengths and salvation, placing perspective on all dimensions of our life with which we have erred on account of our imperfections: *"for all have sinned, and come short of the glory of God" (Romans 3:23)*.

Not always a public display, as in the case of Jesus' crucifixion, our cross is usually the weight imparted to our life, often hidden behind the veil of acts steering our paths, leaving its heavier burden to a mirror image of a weary self: the short Zachariah climbing to catch a glimpse of the approaching Jesus (Luke 19: 1-10), the blind waiting in hope to get in the lake of Bethsaida (John 5:1-15), and the deaf with hopes of hearing (Mark 7:31-37). In spite our concealment behind our defenses, never has the ladder increased a cubit to our heights, the lens improved our sight, nor the microphone our hearing; but in all these we have built towers we cannot reach, exposed lights we cannot see, and sounds we cannot hear, bearing—vices without which we remain who we are—the burdens of the cross we must carry. Consoled, we are never fully comforted by the life of the cross, neither by the lens of the world, but only by the hope of Christ; albeit, belittled in comparison are our burdens to His suffering, perfected for our salvation on the cross.

To demonstrate the meaning of the concept of the cross through physical means, Jesus' occupied His busy agenda on earth guiding the paths of many away from their burdens of the cross. By an invisible Holy Spirit and a well-known God who many have worshiped, but did not believe: *"For the hearts of this people have grown dull, And their ears are hard of hearing, And their eyes they have closed, Lest they should see with their eyes and hear with their ears, Lest they should understand with their hearts and turn, So that I should heal them" (Matthew 13:15)*. Jesus became the personification of deity by whom many would see and believe Him. A representation of physical torture, depravity, temptations, humiliation, and shame, in a sacrificial act through which the downcast were called, healed, comforted, given sight, given life, pardon, and hope, to likewise carry their cross and follow Jesus. Timely, the cross brightly beckoned the final stages of Jesus' release from his earthly duties and eternal freedom from our earthly crosses. In sight, Jesus' means to death was an agonizing pain, that in all humanness, He pleaded to God to forsake, retreating in doubt the pain He's to endure, while many locals wished He would disappear and His closest disciples fell asleep during His most troublesome hour of arrest.

> *refuge in temporal mercies never supplied its share of peace from the conflicts of impending deaths, imminent by our conflicts, to which failure is punishable by death.*

Left to an exercise of faith to strengthen the vessels by which our eyes witness the transformation of our statures, to reach those of the heights of Christ: *"till we come to the unity of the faith and of the knowledge of the Son of God, to a perfect man, to the measure of the stature of the fullness of Christ." (Ephesians 4:11-13),* Jesus promises a soon return to take us with Him. Changing the meaning of our cross from that of shame, to victory, teaching and prophesying of that which edified us to the knowledge of God, in the very cross by which we were once weak. Anecdotal is the remedy which turns our source of pain to that of joy, boastful of the weakness, our minds are refreshed by a spirit of strength, which overcomes the world. Living by the example of the One whose cross became our eyes to the world: *"and be renewed in the spirit of your mind, and that you put on the new man, which was created according to God, in true righteousness and holiness." (Ephesians 4:23).*

By such a bail to life was our lives freed from the sentence of death of which all our imperfections were put to rest on the cross of Jesus. Those imperfections inherited from our fathers, that which we normalized to mere existence, the burdens of our shortcomings, our aimless inquiry to the purpose of life, in which an answer fell short in the eyes of a perfect God. Taking refuge in temporal mercies never supplied its share of peace from the conflicts of impending and continuous deaths, imminent by our conflicts, to which failure is punishable by a hostile verdict to hades, otherwise bypassed through Christ's cross: *"by setting aside in his flesh the law with its commands and regulations. His purpose was to create in himself one new humanity out of the two, thus making peace, and in one body, reconcile both of them to God through the cross, by which he put to death their hostility." (Ephesians 2:15-16).*

The need for a worthy mediator before God to free indebted criminals was carried out on the cross of Jesus, its weight seen in the magnitude by which many had cast their burdens on its bearer, clearing the path to His Holy Spirit that would empower those who died with Him in their cross, to be raised again in Christ. Witnessed by others, the testimony of the history of the cross became an accountability to those who are called out of this world before the end of time when disclosing our return on the investment by the free talent of salvation given on the cross of Jesus will be due.

At the cross roads where one points to life, the other to an unknown destination, many choose the lesser burden to carry, that only short-sightedness trouble sharpens in hind sight by contrast to the more rightful path, perhaps less traveled, pointing back to life of the cross: *"but small is the gate and narrow the road that leads to life, and only a few find it." (Matthew 7:13-14);* for those who are lucky to find will be given the rights to be called the Sons of God.

Battles of the Cross

IX. Death

"O Death where is thy sting? O Hades where is thy victory?"
(1 Corinthians 15:55)

> *On the way, death loses its own sense of boundaries, crossing to those which are not its own, unless it is trampled under the cross of Jesus Christ, where it meets its final defeat.*

IN SHADOWS OF DARKNESS it appears reasonably acceptable to Judas Iscariot to commit suicide for thirty pieces of silver (Matthew 16:15); less desirable a retaliation by Jesus, who would heal the chopped ears of the soldiers that Peter had defensively cut at Gethsemane (John 18:10), preferring to yield to Judas' betrayal arrest to the cross. Jesus and Judas valued life differently, where the latter more readily forsook it, the former pleaded to keep it. In terms of our justice, it was hard for Peter, as well as others, to understand why Jesus stalled His own defense given His powers which He had very well demonstrated to His followers. By standards, not absolute, we eradicate those who harm us, by a strong desire to become the oppressor before we become the oppressed. Some adopt oppression as their defense, undermining the meaning and value to life, many times not for a very high cost—thirty pieces of silver worth. Complacent to the convictions of Jesus' life, Judas valuation to Jesus' more closely aligned with a powerful majority who favored His death, which made his life before the truth, which he had witnessed being a disciple of Jesus, unbearable in the eyes of God, as well as, his own. Yet Judas' death wasn't a direct intervention of God, but an indirect choice by Judas, displaying a striking difference between the judgement of God and those of men, who choose the works of Satan over God.

Death, therefore, reigned in humanity, beginning with Adam, and incessantly repeated by Cain and Abel, staged magnanimously in world wars, eradications, and famines, that have shamefully displayed the evil desires of man's judgement when executed away from the word of God, that the new Adam—Jesus Christ—would reverse by His resurrection. Recalcitrant to discipline by the word of God, death devours life on the premise of the absence of God, challenging His wisdom to the future by taking wrathful measures to control the present pain. On the way, death loses its own sense of boundaries, crossing to those which are not its own, unless it is trampled under the cross of Jesus Christ, where it meets its final defeat.

Victory it has become, from the symbol of defeat, death's sting has been changed. By comfort and assurance inspired by the consoling spirit of God in a promise of reuniting with those who are separated from us again in Christ; in Jesus who's been given power over death, who reunites the spirits of those who in Him die: "*Then shall the dust return to the earth as it was: and the spirit shall return unto God who gave it.*" (*Ecclesiastes 12:7*), to be resurrected again with Him upon His return. Those who are faithful will draw their lives around the word of God, becoming the living word through faith. By righteousness, the Holy Spirit will replace uncertainties and fears of death, with fears of the One in whose hands are the keys of life, whose powers transcend over life and death, who has His full knowledge of our destinies. Die not like the world then, but like sons of God, concerned with His kingdom in heaven, not of the things of this world.

> "*just as sin reigned in death, so also grace might reign through righteousness, to bring eternal life through Jesus Christ, our Lord*" (*Romans 5:21*).

By no greater agent of life has death been defeated than by the love of Christ, who annulled our temporary, decaying earthly temples, sentenced to death, with the permanent robes of life by which He had destined us from the womb, to be brothers and sisters of Christ: "*But we see Jesus, who was made a little lower than the angels, for the suffering of death crowned with glory and honor, that He, by the grace of God, might taste death for everyone.*" (Hebrews 2:9). Often lost to a worldlier wisdom, such a prescription to life defiles the definitions by which death had slowly creeped to normalcy of our psyches as a mere end to all matter, inconsiderate of evidence to its defeat by those who—following the resurrection of Jesus—denied it its powers. Others who have ascribed to death's immanency, spiritually separated themselves from their first love—Christ—by whom they must reestablish their relationship: "*so that, just as sin reigned in death, so also grace might reign through righteousness, to bring eternal life through Jesus Christ, our Lord*" (Romans 5:21). Bound by any other truth to eternal life is not of God. Implying indebtedness to the world's doctrinal and spiritual death, the remediation message of the cross of Jesus is replaced by a verdict of death. Plausible in the eyes of a merciful God to put an end to a perpetual endemic of man's laws of death by a perfect man's death to life: "*for the perishable must be clothed with the imperishable, and the mortal with immortality. When the perishable has been clothed with the imperishable and the mortal with immortality, then the saying that is written will come to pass: "Death has been swallowed up in victory*" (1 Corinthians 15:53-53), that in all things we give Him the glory for our gift of life.

Returning to the wrathful paths of man by denial of the gift of life, we find God's mercies are overshadowed by other boundaries of men who have retired life to experiment with God's vengeance. Where God's patient mercies have abounded, so has our defiance to His sovereignty, which He venerated through death. Hence, our verdict to the death is the ignorance by which we are blinded to our destiny, like Judas Iscariot, manifested in a choice away from life. It is no surprise, the extreme measure of degradation endured by Jesus Christ in the face of persecutions, to set a new example by which we become a testimony to the mercies of God, who had chosen the sacrifice of His Son over our destruction, that in contrast, the vileness of wrathful death in the man-made laws of sin are abolished forever: *"I have been crucified with Christ and I no longer live, but Christ lives in me. The life I now live in the body, I live by faith in the Son of God, who loved me and gave himself for me."* (Galatians 2:20)

> *to some, however; the abrupt ending of death to an incomplete list of questions about life, suffices the moments they live.*

Beginning the day in which we're born, death is at work in the flesh, which it spirited heartedly before Jesus Christ was resurrected. We decay to the physical laws imposed on us, with many attempts to escape its toll, all of which fail in the unexplainable abruptness of death *"for we are aliens and pilgrims before you, as were all our fathers, our days on earth are as a shadow, and without hope."* (1 Chronicles 29:15). While becoming inseparable from the meaning of life by the unforgivable laws of nature, our denial of it has been granted by the life and resurrection of Jesus Christ, that the cyclical seasons have come to demonstrate nothing more than the nearness and the hope of Christ's return. Detaching from our peddling relationships with others, death marks our wrathful and rebellious nature by which we entangle others, that we aspire as a final discontinuation to all things that we deem undesirable. In the flesh, death's unfolding moments place tremendous hope on things borrowed from an imagination of a future that doesn't materialize away from the grave. Spiritually, dying is the suspension from the sudden drop of life which we have climbed on the premise of the "two birds on the tree", leaving the dreamier selves to those spiritualists who sought a greater meaning out of life in the word of God—dying to life in the flesh—they live on the assurance of the "one bird at hand".

IX. Death

Carving a path to death with a rosier outlook, they engage in unimaginable feats of destruction, who like Judas, were betrayed by the fleeting birds they never managed to prey. For both, in the flesh and in the spirit, the omnipotent laws of nature are rarely broken except through the divine intervention of Jesus Christ, and His triumphant resurrection. In Him was found the perfect balance of the flesh and spirit, by whom life has been gifted to those who believed in His salvation: *"Verily, verily, I say unto you, if a man keeps my commandment, he shall never see death." (John 8:51).* To some, however; the abrupt ending of death to an incomplete list of questions about life suffices the moment they live.

X. Resurrection

"I know that my Savior lives, and at the end He will stand
on this earth. My flesh may be destroyed, yet from this
body I will see God."
(Job 19:25-26)

"Because He lives, I can face tomorrow.
Because He lives, all fear is gone
Because I know, I know, He holds the future
And Life is worth a living
Just because He lives."
–Gloria and William Gaither

> *Jesus' resurrection demonstrates a scientific*
> *breakthrough in biological and medicinal do-*
> *mains of surgical reparation to severely dislo-*
> *cated body.*

SUCH POWERFUL LYRICS TO a beautiful hymn promising divine
assurance to life, granted by the resurrection of Jesus Christ.
Restoring autonomy to the body of Christ—both spiritually and
physically—reviving hopes to Jesus' followers and disciples who've
been promised a similar resurrection to that which they've witnessed in Christ. Being helpless spectators to His crucifixion, with
faint hopes His promised return will be fulfilled, Jesus' reappear-
ance in the flesh was met with great disbelief by some who had
to touch His nail-scarred hands to believe Him. Nevertheless,
"Rejoice!" (Matthew 28:9), Jesus said to His disciples before they

witnessed His ascension, promising an arrival of another proxy who would take His place in consoling their efforts to spread the message of salvation to the world, like He did when He was with them. No more in the flesh, the Holy Spirit became the backbone by which faith would be extended to Christ's body represented in the church: *"Now you are the body of Christ, and each one of you is a part of it." (1 Corinthians 12:27),* fulfilling God's plan since creation to eternally overcome the verdict of death that had been introduced by sin since the beginning of creation. By His resurrection, Jesus becomes the first to defeat death, putting away its "sting" to all who would believe in Him: *"But now Christ is risen from the dead, and has become the first fruits of those who have fallen asleep. For since by man came death, by Man also came the resurrection of the dead. For as in Adam all die, even so in Christ all shall be made alive. But each one in his own order: Christ the first fruits, afterward those who are Christ's at His coming."* 1 Cor. 15:20-23.

The resurrection of Jesus Christ carries many significances, accentuating its spiritual relevance to our immortality, most notable is the physical implications represented in the regeneration of life from death, that in the example given by Jesus, the body was fully restored, demonstrating a scientific breakthrough in biological and medicinal domains of surgical reparation to severely dislocated body, after undergoing extreme physical trauma similar to that of the crucifix. Comparable only to out-of-body experiences and surreal dreams of multiple timely dimensions, resurrection reaffirms our spiritual awareness of that which is outside of us, perceivable by the intricate labyrinth of our brain as the agent of communication, in which our bodies are a mere instrument to the Spirit of God residing inside of us, alive, regenerating our bodies to life. Having accelerated Jesus' healing after the cross, God's Holy Spirit, would likewise, bring together His body—the church—to revive and to heal. Notwithstanding any losses to its members, God sought a full recovery of the entire body of Jesus, therefore; reviving all of its members under His authority, as the Head. While such a phenomenon surpasses our most advanced and sophisticated techniques by all standards, as Jesus' three-day burial would have medically disqualified His decayed body for any revivals, it is a phenomenon to be reckoned with given its rare occurrence in man's history, none of which were lead to a divine heavenly ascension like Christ's. Put together, the hypothetical culmination of all living brains alive today would not enable such a capability to the extent exhibited in Christ's resurrection, that at best, may only find its closest imitation in sci-fi movies about a fabricated future.

Nevertheless, our denial of resurrection represents the most egregious negligence to impendent possibilities of a magnitude that is equivalent to the paralysis imposed by the loss of communication between the head and the body, represented by God and His Church in Jesus Christ.

> ... *the minds of the people had been leavened with heresies denying the monumental work done by God through Jesus, leading to the resurrection of His body.*

Jesus' resurrection revitalized much needed presence of an invisible God to a creation too caught-up in death avoidance, that have paralyzed essential pathways to constituencies of life characteristic of the more spiritual aspects of communication between God and His church, represented in the body of Christ. Many who find solace in the independence of the self from a spiritual being, diffuse the significance of coherence found in the body to the reliance on an evolutionary chance over any constraint by a concept of God, debilitating vital spiritual supplies to a much tacit peripherals, vying for their gradual decay.

Having eased away from the explicit laws of morality earlier instilled by Moses, more implicit laws made lenient, both, the admission to eternal life, as well as, a subtle and deteriorating spiritual death that was a result of the numerous evasions to repentance by the cross of Jesus. By those doubtful Thomas' requiring proof (John 20:19), overlooked by many of Jesus prosecutors, the minds of the people had been leavened with heresies denying the monumental work done by God through Jesus, leading to the resurrection of His body. In spite of continuous efforts to suppress Jesus' power, God pursues further restoration with us, sending His Spirit to complete the witness of the ascension of His Son to Heaven by His disciples, becoming the proxies by which autonomy is restored to the body of Christ.

Promising much life to those spiritually dead, we find the Holy Spirit's work in its regenerative capacity to restore the self to Jesus Christ to be the spinal cord of our salvation, bridging the "free-willed" body members back with God, the head of our faith. Resurrecting all members to His body, God restored all creation to Himself by demonstrating the value He placed in each one of us to be a vital member in the Body of Christ: *"I am the resurrection, and the life; he that believeth on me, though he dies, yet shall he live."* *(John 11:25)*.

XI. Power

"Serve the Lord with fear and rejoice with trembling. Kiss the son, lest He be angry, and you perish in the way, when His wrath is kindled but a little. Blessed are all those who put their trust in Him."
(Psalm 2:11-12)

> *. . . another form of power more conducive to our survival and longevity than the apocalypse-like wrath He wishes to do away with, is the referent power of love.*

POWERFUL WERE GOD'S WORDS to King Hezekiah through the prophet Isaiah against Sennacherib King of Assyria, reprimanding him for blaspheming against the Lord, and avowing to never allow him to enter Jerusalem by slaughtering 185,000 soldiers in the Assyrian camp: *"Who is it you have ridiculed and blasphemed? Against whom have you raised your voice and lifted your eyes in pride?" (Isaiah 37:23)*. An epic disaster to a tipping point in God's judgement against a proud an idolatrous nation challenging His power and might. In prior examples, God prolonged negotiations have led to recurring plagues in the fleeing camps of a chased people in the desert, exhausting all attempts to peaceable departure of Israel out of the land of Egypt, without incurring such a heavy human toll on a nation. Like the sovereignty of nations, God demands respectful worship in awe and fear of His ultimate power over all, as an enlightenment to a less informed creation with which He wishes to establish a lasting covenant of peace. While ignorance of the unknown intercedes for short comings, not much can be done with informed, blatant, and the self-arrogance shown in the example of Sennacherib. Slowly arousing the anger of a rather merciful God, is the irreversible discourse that may have resulted from misreading the road signs to God's sovereignty. To buffer such a prevalent state of delusion about His might, God would introduce another form of power more conducive to our survival and longevity than the apocalypse-like wrath He wishes to do away with, that which can be achieved through the referent power of love.

Nevertheless, some like King Saul preferred coercion over referent power. To eradicate any possible threats to his throne and eliminate any doubtful betrayal by his son Jonathan with David, King Saul used violent coercion to spear his son and repeatedly attempted the murder of King David. After an unsuccessful lethal chase, few hundred soldiers were killed and a terminal suicide by King Saul on mount Gilboa, following the death of his son Jonathan by the Philistines, concluded a rather violent pursuit of power by King Saul. Saul's death was the result of numerous erratic decisions in his pursuit of power that have aroused the Lord's anger against him. One of which was his consultation with spiritual mediums to call on the Prophet Samuel's spirit from the dead to reassure him of his throne, the very act that informed him of his upending death.

By contrast, a subtler referent pursuit to power is shown in the story of Naomi and Ruth, brought together to sustain life through a difficult period after losing both their husbands to death: *"Entreat me not to leave thee, or to return from following after thee; for whither thou goest, I will go, and where thou lodgest, I will lodge. Thy people shall be my people, and thy God my God." (Ruth 1:16).* Ruth did not leave Naomi during a difficult time, which Naomi perceived as the Lord's punishment, when she said: *"call me Mara: For the Almighty hath dealt very bitterly with me. I went out full, and the Lord hath brought me home again empty" (Ruth 1:13)* in response to God's possible intervention to redirect her back from the idolatrous land of Moab to Bethlehem. A powerful reversal of Naomi and Ruth's destiny is seen in the marriage of Boaz to Ruth.

God's blessed their lives, having gifted them with their son Obed who would become the grandfather to the household of Jesse, and his son King David whom the Lord greatly blessed, and made him a leader of his people Israel, from whose descendant the promise of Jesus was fulfilled.

Proving most ineffective, coercive power seen in our historic wars and ongoing battles reflect on our rather violent nature and our preferences to coercion as the means to power. Unsustainable, Jesus' came to earth to do exactly the opposite of coercion by choosing the more difficult painful path to the cross. Jesus would demonstrate the power of His love by dying for those who would believe in Him to save them to eternal life: *"I am the way, the truth, and the life; no one comes to the Father except through me." John 14:6.* Tempted, Jesus did not yield to trials by Satan who attempted to steer Him to the lure of earthly kingdoms that he promised to forsake if Jesus would bow to him. Aware of his wrathful schemes, Jesus denied his attempts to test the Lord, who by a later power over death would forever change their means to power, and return all authority in heaven and earth to Jesus. Empowered by God, Jesus is resurrected, putting the last enemy of humanity—death—to rest. In powerful truth, the word of God shows struggles of many who in their pursuits to attain power, lost a valuable relationship with God, whose mercies have been the most powerful tool of His judgments. While others, more attuned to the God's words, achieve appreciable outcomes by their show of reverence and awe to the many powerful works of God, by which Jesus is crowned.

Showing a more compassionate path to power, Jesus shares the parable of the Good Samaritan (Luke 10:25), where stepping out of the way for others can be very powerful. The Samaritan's choice to help the stricken stranger on the road, was greatly rewarded in heaven, as Jesus indicated. Later he points to the poor widow who put the two mites of offering in the temple (Luke 21:1) tithing all she had, in sign of powerful belief in sufficient provision of Lord to life. Moreover, Jesus' powerful parables, reiterated more strongly by His death and resurrection, remains a valuable example that is divine in nature, that many who have sought to achieve it, found His powerful miracles itinerant with His compassionate character, by which His works of healing were of secondary significance to the exceptional servant-like leadership He primed His disciples to imitate. Witnessed, even in His zealous wrath over merchant trading in God's temple, turning their tables outside the temple, Jesus stirred the crowds to the more suitable trades of God in His place of worship, separating the things of Caesar's from those of the God, He strongly demonstrated His fervent will to maintain God's place of worship to the gifts and spiritual talents He bestowed on His disciples, empowering them to continue His legacy of servant power.

By similar denial of the "I" to that witnessed in Jesus, the ego which sought to enforce a powerful risk to the survival of a vital interdependence given in the examples of Saul and David, Naomi and Ruth, demands a more controllable power over the will, attained from God. Power examples are given in the parables Jesus shared with His followers, demonstrating compassion to servitude as an alternative to the short-lived, coercive powers otherwise preferred by the ways of the world. Anointed by God through the Holy Spirit, we are reminded that: "*Not by might nor by power, but by my Spirit,' says the Lord Almighty.*" (*Zechariah 4:6*). As we seek God's power through the Holy Spirit we will also be given the peace of God promised by His Son Jesus Christ: "*Peace I leave with you, my peace I give to you: not as the world giveth, do I give unto you. Let not your heart be troubled, nor let it be afraid.*" (*John 14:27*). Likewise, our renewed hope to power must change to that of God's will: "*But you will receive power when the Holy Spirit comes on you; and you will be my witnesses in Jerusalem, and in all Judea and Samaria, and to the ends of the earth.*" (*Acts 1:8*).

XII. Prayer

*"Therefore I say to you whatever things you ask when you
pray, believe that you receive them, and you will have
them."*
(Mark 11:24)

"THIS IS MY BELOVED *Son in whom I'm well pleased"* (Matthew
3:17) was God's voice that came from heaven to mark the very
special occasion of His son's baptism. Rare are the occasions in
the Bible where God's voice is heard from Heaven—usually in
the presence of His Son Jesus—witnessed only by few anointed
people, whom He chose to represent Him to the world, or during
a revelation to the magnitude of giving the ten commandment to
Moses. If it were to recur today, God's voice would probably cause
a catastrophic havoc, sounding a promised return of His Son Jesus
Christ. Apart from the challenges, few, if any, were counted worthy
to stand before God, whose powerful countenance is comparable
to the sun, causing John, James, and Peter to fall faced down to
the ground during Jesus' transfiguration on the mountain. Too
noisy to hear, the world makes faint the voice of God spoken by
the Holy Spirit through His word. More challenging is a having
a conversation with a God who knows everything and is aware
of everything without hearing His voice through the Holy Spirit.
Seeking mercy not sacrifice, the Lord delights in our humble voice
that acknowledges Him as our Lord and King, above all else in our
lives. To quiet the world in order to hear the continuous whispers
of the Holy Spirit in our ears, is the only indication of a livelihood
dialogue with God; all the "rest" God provides: *"But seek ye first the*

kingdom of God, and his righteousness; and all these things shall be added unto you." (Matthew 6:33).

Before turning to idols and arousing the Lord's anger against Him, by prayers King Solomon sought the counsel of the Lord in wisdom. Pleased was the Lord with His prayer request, that He blessed Him with incredible riches to wisdom and knowledge that many have come to admire. Heeding efforts to build a dedicated temple to God, King Solomon anointed the Jerusalem temple where the Lord chose to reside among His people where He would show His love and support to them. But God doesn't reside in temples made by hands, for the earth is His footstool and the Heavens is His throne; God seeks to dwell in the temples of our hearts and minds. Occupied with other idols, we obstruct God's Spirit from pleading to our souls to remove all that separates us from Him. Anointed, God has chosen the life of Solomon to be the vessels by which His Holy Spirit communes with His people in prayers, that by their active dialogue, they've come to hear and learn the will and wisdom of God: *"If my people who are called by My name will humble themselves, and pray and seek My face, and turn from their wicked ways, then I will hear from heaven, and will forgive their sin and heal their land." (2 Chronicles 7:1)* were God's words to Solomon. It must have been a great disappointment to God when King Solomon turned to idol worship later in life, arousing the Lord's anger against him before Solomon died, albeit; leaving exemplary legacy rich in all aspects of knowledge and wisdom that many would remember to this day as a testimony to the power of relationships with God through prayers.

> *While it's hard to imagine any relationship based only on needs, thankfully God's capacity towards us is far greater than ours towards Him . . .*

Compared to lilies and ravens, Solomon's in all of His glory did not fair like one these, as we later learn from Jesus. Sent by

God, Jesus' hoped to achieve a more perfect example than that of Solomon, reaching many with little or no access to resources, in wisdom or riches, He used the much simpler creations of lilies and birds to demonstrate the powerful complexities of God's wisdom. Birds and flower do not toil or harvest, yet not one of them fall without the knowledge of God: *"Look at the birds of the air, for they neither sow nor reap nor gather into barns; yet your heavenly Father feeds them. Are you not of more value than they?" (Matthew 6:26).* Derailed, however; later dialogues with Solomon failed, requiring a greater intervention than mere temple dedication. Prayers were in shortage. Distracted by God's blessing, His people strayed to other idols to present sacrifices to, stirring Him to anger. Jesus' disciples were similarly distracted by concerns over a loaf of bread for their boat journey with Jesus, after He had miraculously prayed to feed a group of four thousand with only seven loaves of bread, picking up seven baskets of leftover fragments. It is evident that we are in need of continuous prayers to overcome the short-term memory from which we all suffer, often forgetting the evident grace and mercies of God in our lives. No longer is our prayers about dialogue with God, but about requests to demands of the flesh. While it's hard to imagine any relationship based only on needs, thankfully God's capacity towards us is far greater than ours towards Him, that He delights in our brief, self-centered focus of our lives which we present to Him in prayers.

God is a living being, unlike idols and inanimate objects; He responds to our pleas and requests. Indications about God speak to His omnipresence, most evident in our personal experiences and testimonies with Him that are a direct result of our conversations in prayers, in which His responses are readily witnessed in our lives. Some, on the other hand, seem to have discovered a rare quality in other idols, out-of-character with God, often put in place of God. Most idols are mute; they do not talk back at us, making our relationship to them a one-way road in which desire is the main driver. Unlike our two-way relationship with God, where listening and speaking are vital indications of a lively dialogue about an ongoing relationship with Him. Our God-like egos interject to

anything that goes against our will, however. "Thou shall not create any other Gods before me" was a difficult a command to obey
by Solomon, from a God who had numerously helped him and his
people build a great kingdom, when later Solomon defaulted to
building altars for other idols and gods that were worshipped by
the tribes and nations among whom they dwelled.

The word of God demonstrated a nation in constant state of
disarray away from its creator, that in spite of God's intervention
to help them, they turn around and disobey him: David's triumph
over Goliath with a sling and a stone, the tumbling of Jericho's
walls, and numerous victorious battles against the Philistines,
Amorites, Moabites, and Hittites that speak to God's promise to
"lands flowing with milk and honey" (Deuteronomy 27) standing on
His promises to His people: *"For He is good, For His mercy endures
Forever." (Psalms 136:1).* Undermining the guiding pillars of fire
by night and the shadows of clouds by day, out of Egypt, God's
people deferred their worship, finding the adherence to the ten
commandment tabloid difficult to keep, built golden Baals to worship, that short of a human remediation, it was almost impossible
to convey the significance of their rebellion towards God. Short
of an avowal of faith in a prayer by His people, God determines
the sacrifice must be of a magnitude equivalent to their separation
from Him, whose judgments must remit the guilt of the multitudes who disobeyed Him, perhaps by an intervention that would
reestablish their relationship and prayer communication between
Him and them.

> *The genuine soul that truly seeks God's will,
> does not seek what is for itself, but has full trust
> in the will of God*

Sent to teach among others, Jesus remediates communication
to God by the Lord's prayers, which He ordains to supplement our
pleas with God. Not boastful, but in private, unlike the long rituals
of temple prayers at the time, Jesus instructs us to "ask" and "seek"

in prayers (Matthew 7:10), with faith, the assurance of our relationship with God, when we ask Him humbly and in accordance to His will, we hear His answer. In righteousness—for evil thoughts, He despises—we approach Him with a pure heart, *"for the eyes of the Lord are on the righteous; His ears are open to their prayers"* (1 Peter 3:12), having forgiven the "trespasses" of others—seventy times seven—by His power of the Holy Spirit, overcome our rather ill wishes upon others and their lives, and the pain they may have caused us, before we enter in conversation with God. Remembering the crucifix and Jesus' deep distress on the cross, as such our patience in prayers must be: *"You have not yet resisted to bloodshed, striving against sin."* (Hebrews 12:4), there is the faith in prayers that seeks God's will before ours, believing that His promises are in due time: *"And all these, having obtained a good testimony through faith, did not receive the promise, God having provided something better for us, that they should not be made perfect apart from us."* (Hebrews 11:39-40). The genuine soul that truly seeks God's will, does not seek what is for itself, but has full trust in the will of God; that was well demonstrated by Jesus' prayers in the garden of Gethsemane, when He prayed: *"My Father, if it be possible, let this cup pass from me; nevertheless, not as I will, but as you will." (Matthew 26:39).*

Unlike babies only occupied with their needs, prayers are a continuous work in progress requiring discernment—a familiarity with the voice of God—to the knowledge of the heart of the Lord, which comes from a relationship that grows with Him. With diligence we learn to hear the voice of God in our prayers, away from the more self-focused desires of self-fulfillment. Not of novice acquaintance, our partnership with God is a testimony of our prayers, reflecting more strongly on our relationship with Him than with that of the world: *"Brothers and sisters, I could not address you as people who live by the Spirit, but as people who are still worldly—mere infants in Christ. I gave you milk, not solid food, for you were not yet ready for it. Indeed, you are still not ready. You are still worldly. For since there is jealousy and quarreling among you, are you not worldly? Are you not acting like mere humans?" (1 Corinthians 3: 1-3).*

> *Prayer is the practice of communication with God to learn of His ultimate desires for us to first seek His kingdom. We all testify to God's countless blessings in our lives ...*

Prayer is the practice of communication with God to learn of His ultimate desires for us to first seek His kingdom. We all testify to God's countless blessings in our lives: through nourishment, in times of hunger, in healing, in times of sickness, in blessings during times of need, in successes in life, through acknowledgement and praise, in happiness, in fulfillment, in great, and small, God's blessings are countless towards us. Prayer refocuses our intentions to the things which God desires. It is the means by which the awareness of our needs is belittled before God. In prayers, God allows us, through the Holy Spirit, to express how we feel about our lives, perhaps reaffirming His own feelings about the same things we pray about, or correcting our false perceptions about things that hinder our relationship with Him. When we pray, we acknowledge our need for a change, we ask God to intervene in our lives to bring about the best change possible for a predicament or a situation. Prayers done in faith, with pure motives and confidence in God's mercy, are always answered. We approach God in prayer by repentance of our hearts and minds, from all evil desires present in our lives: *"Wash yourselves, make yourselves clean; put away the evil of your doings from before My eyes. Cease to do evil, learn to do good; seek justice, rebuke the oppressor; defend the fatherless, plead for the widow. "Come now and let us reason together," Says the Lord, "Through your sins are like scarlet, they shall be as white as snow; though they are red like crimson, they shall be as wool." (Isaiah 1:16-18).* Learning to hear His voice and have discernment in our prayers to stand before God is crucial to opening His ears to our pleas and our hearts to His voice. "Praying without ceasing", is no longer a human effort, but an inspired, ongoing dialogue between our hearts and that of the Father's. Done according to His will, prayers become a witness to the ways God is present in our lives, and a testimony to His answered prayers: *"if a son asks for bread from any father among you, will he give him a stone? Or if he asks for a fish, will he give him a serpent instead of a fish?" (Luke 11:11).*

XII. Prayer

Lord Jesus Christ:

Creator of everything, in heaven and on earth, all mighty God, perfect in knowledge and wisdom above our understanding. Thank you for the opportunity of calling us your children. Lord we believe in your words and will to our lives as your children. Like you promised in Ezekiel: "That they may walk in My statutes and keep My judgments and do them; and they shall be My people, and I will be their God." (Ezekiel 11:20), and so we bow before you in prayer seeking your will in our lives. It is through your blessed son, our Lord and Savior, Jesus Christ, whom you have given power and authority over everything that is in heaven and on earth; for through Him alone we are justified to lift our prayers to you, to stand and behold you in all of your glory. In gratefulness to your everlasting mercies and love that you have eternally unveiled to all your children, we thank you. We thank you for the Holy Spirit and its awesome and wonderful work in us. Lord Jesus, I pray that you answer our pleas to be Holy presentable and without blemish to God the Father. That you forgive our short-sighted arrogance and our limited knowledge of our self-centered selfish desires, often in the way of our paths to You. May your intercessions for us cover Satan's bad reports persistently on your children. There in our best, and in our worst, we realize how vain our lives are when compared with the riches and the glories you have for all those who call upon your name. I would like to ask your patience on our difficult and slowly changing selves, that through longsuffering you teach us the true meaning of living by which you have personally paid a precious price for us to salvation and the inheritance of your heavenly kingdom. I pray that you provide us with new insights to the fulfillment of our time here on earth, as it is in heaven. In spite of your powerful revelation and presence in our lives, our relationship with you has increasingly distanced the world from us, when we realize how much more worthy it is to spend our lives for you. How unacceptable a merit is our lives in comparison to your sacrificial story of salvation, that many a wise have failed to acknowledge it, yet in your unfathomable wisdom you have revealed it to children. Help us the coming time to better manage the things that we should do, with the knowledge that it is all to your glory: "But let all those rejoice who put their trust in You, let them ever shout for joy, because You defend them; let those who love Your name be joyful in You". Help us through our imperfections and those of the world, through trials and tribulations that ensnare our lives as we draw nearer to you. Help us accept the certainty of your eternal life, even to the fleeting corruption of death, and the insignificance of all things that are not a part of you. I pray that our boast will be of Your closeness by the cross to our lives, that in all things present and future, You are the center. May our prayers through words and action, in mind, heart, body, soul, and spirit become the fulfillment of your plan for our lives. As we learn through life, may your narrow paths be edged by the chariots of your wisdom, as it guides through to eternal reconciliation with ourselves and with God. Help us in the coming tribulations to lean on nothing else but on the power of your Holy Spirit, for we cannot do it on our own, but with every word that comes out of the mouth the Lord through the eternal knowledge of our Lord and Savior, Jesus Christ, to Him be all the glory forever. Amen.

XIII. Praise

"I charge you O daughter of Jerusalem, by the gazelles or
by the deer of the field, do not stir up nor awaken love
until it pleases."
(Song of Solomon 2:7)

Sound may have mattered little to God, much
more the heart that uttered it. No greater joy
has God remembered His people by than dur-
ing their moments of praise.

BEFORE THE MORE ELABORATE expression of praise existed, in
music, poetry, or other forms, a simpler "thank you" expressing a
heart full of gratitude found various forms in expressions of praise,
in all tongues, tribes and nations. Many out of awe had discovered sounds that they found pleasing tones to be pervasively re-
producible by winds, strings, drums, and many more instruments
designed as expression of praise. King David dedicated the book
of Psalms to God's praise by using lyrical poetry, which many have
used in praise by putting music to. Written with gratitude, praise is
the intent of keeping a continuous thankfulness to the greatness of
God. Sound may have mattered little to God, much more the heart
that uttered it. No greater joy has God remembered His people
by than during their moments of praise. Empowered, the voice of
trumpets brought down the walls of Jericho (Joshua 6:2-16). Powerful, was the Spirit of God which descended in tongues of fire
on the apostles (Acts 2:3) when they got together to praise God.

Much humbler was the praise at Jesus' reception on the colt to Jerusalem, when the crowd cheered Him: "Hosanna in the highest"; much more glorious will be His praise when He returns, likely to overshadow our most cherished praises of those by Handel's "Hallelujah Chorus" or Bach's momentous cantatas. In all of its forms, praise to God awakens the love we have with Him, very much like the passion expressed between lovers in the Song of Solomon, known to symbolize Christ's love for his bride, the Church.

Mary praised the Spirit that made her pregnant. The three kings praised baby Jesus in the manger. The heavens praised when out of the water Jesus came. The leper praised Jesus for his skin; the lame for his legs, the withered hands for their vitality, and the dead for life. In awe they praised Jesus with Elijah and Moses on the mountain. She praised Jesus when her shame was covered. Released his tongue, the mute praised Jesus. Calming the seas, the disciples praised Jesus. In praise, Jesus walked on water; by praise Peter was not drowned. The widow received all the praise for the two mites she offered. The multitude praised a twelve basket of left over fragment that was made from five loaves of bread. By expensive spikenard, Martha praised Jesus' feet. Healed of her bleeding a woman crawled to praise Jesus. In praise the lame carried His bed and walked. The blind praised the light that opened his eyes.

Deriving much pleasure from their praise, God goes to extraordinary measures to the lost sheep, that heavens praises over the ninety-nine in the field; He sells all he has, in praise of the one pearl, worth all.

Awakened, God's love through praise fulfills His glory, graceful as the gazelle's trotting in the open field, like the wind, it moves to its destiny. So our hearts move when we praise the creator, the One who called them His own: "*everyone who is called by my name, whom I created for my glory, whom I formed and made.*" (*Isaiah 43:7*).

So "*Make a joyful shout to God, all the earth! Sing out the honor of His name; make His praise glorious.*" (Psalms 66:1), for soon He shall take the chaff away bringing home the crop.

XIV. Justice

"Knowing that a man is not justified by the works of the law, but by faith in Jesus Christ, even we have believed in Christ Jesus, that we might be justified by faith. In Christ and not by the works of the law, for by the works of the law no flesh shall be justified."
(Galatians 2:16)

Before it became too abstract by many deeds, justice established on perfect law became the pursuit of many who based their understanding on the word of God.

TENDING TO THE LAWS of the universe governing our physical world, we discover domains held by an impeccable balance, including those of our bodies, by which we have gained insights to the concepts and laws of justice. Acquiring consistency by the constants of nature, we've experimented with applications of physical laws that have given us walking domains to the skies, defying gravity; a spectral lens to the invisible lights that have accelerated our notions of perception, growing in knowledge and wisdom about the matters that make us. Not found on the short immediacy of our desires, however; wisdom to knowledge accumulated over time, when understanding of our behavior became an innate response to the natural imbalances we've become aware of after the fall of Adam. A greater means of governance necessitated controls to an otherwise non-human, impulse driven creations, whose precepts to justices are a theocracy of covetous imbalances to fleshly needs, leaving adherences of the convoluted laws of justice to the savvier interpreters, capitalizing from their imbalances. Left to man, stern applications of law implied favoritism by those who control it, fornicating with the deeds and desires of the general public, that in all systems of law, tipping it to one man's favor has always been the aim. Justice became less about maintaining balance, more about adjustment to new lights, that prior to the tipping point, have not been exposed to our judicial lens. Encompassing most acts, justice falls short to deeds undefined outside the terms of law of known violations, leading to the evolution of alternatives—a social practice of adopted norms—remediating justice by agreement to those impacted by it. A popular route to justice in modern day infractions between parties without involvement of the justice system, frequently practiced by earlier justices, has established means to legality that later morphed into laws.

Before it became too abstract by many deeds, justice established on perfect law became the pursuit of many who based their understanding on the word of God: *"He is the Rock, his works are perfect, and all his ways are just. A faithful God who does no wrong, upright and just is He" (Deuteronomy 32:4)*. Unbiased, God's words and judgment were explicitly stated in ten commandments, by which most acts and deeds were classified. With man in consideration, God's laws favored a nation by whom He made His laws, by which He became bound to its fulfillment irrespective of its application: *"Therefore you shall obey the voice of the Lord your God, and observe His commandments and His statutes which I command you today." (Deuteronomy 27:10)*. Claiming absolute power over the nations, God holds the law of man, who would soon violate it by deeds that he would argue as the non-negotiable, perfect scepter of God.

> *Unwise it may seem to some that: "wisdom is justified by all her children" (Luke 7:35)*

XIV. Justice

In the non-selective adoption of God's law, one unconditionally accepts all of its applications, unambiguous in its intent by the most popular volume of moral codes in man's history, from which many legal systems and religions have emerged today. In its less restricted relative of morals, however; a more degenerate form of behavior replaces the eloquence of lawful acts by a practical application, which some have implored to an abridged version of a judicial subsystems exercised in less complex social circles, expanding on similar motifs of the law of God, more bounded by a free-will to religious atheism. Retiring all possibilities of achieving perfection, we transition justice by the word of God to the morals of society, to achieve justification of acts normalized by the majority, maintaining reasonable acts as a minimum requirement while preserving a "no condemnation" frontier from others. When it's unlawful to lie, it's not immoral to "tell a white lie"; "murder" is unlawful but "cannibalism" to some is not immoral; "cursing" is unlawful but "gossip" is not immoral. In the judgement of man, justice is achieved through the law; in the judgement of God, justice is achieved by the time continuum of law and morals, through all acts known to man, to which He's established a covenant, in His word, silencing the argument about "nature vs. nurture" through a perfect law that governs all behaviors. "It is written: thou shall put no other God before me" cannot be moralized by creating a Baal, or an image thereof, to worship; nor is "though shall love the Lord thy God with all your heart and soul" be replaced by a moralized "love to our neighbors", even if that's a close second in commands of importance.

Unwise it may seem to some that: *"wisdom is justified by all her children" (Luke 7:35)*, the implementation of unalterable Godly justice system by which explicit human acts are condemned, finding its pleas for a change futile before a God whose laws are not retractable. Many erred to tailor their own derivative, man-made laws, more suited to their acts: *"So they left all the commandments of the Lord their God, made for themselves a molded image and two calves, made a wooden image and worshiped all the host of heaven and served Baal. And they caused their sons and daughters* to pass through the fire, practiced witchcraft and soothsaying, and sold themselves to do evil in the sight of the Lord, to provoke Him to anger." (2 Kings 17:16-17). When faced with Godly justice, a degenerate law exercised by man lead to destruction, while execution seemed a more reasonable resolution by a pardoning God, seeking justice by sacrificing His Son becomes a remedial act by Jesus—the advocate—through whom God's justice system would be appeased: *"knowing that a man is not justified by the works of the law, but by faith in Jesus Christ, even we have believed in Christ Jesus, that we might be justified by faith in Christ and not by the works of the law; for by the works of the law no flesh shall be justified." (Galatians 2:12)*

I, therefore, managed my life around keeping man's law, taken to remediation through peaceable resolutions when erred and condemned. Through good works and deeds of faith in God—and as a Christian—in Jesus Christ, I learned God's commandments and words, in timely spiritual maturity by discernment and revelations from the word of God, inspiring all good works: in displays of kindness through the respect of others' lives—theirs, as well as my own—in honoring my oaths, in speaking truth to authorities, without unsettled violations, with the best of intentions, towards the growing bond between morals and justice. I await, on the other hand, the verdict on many common unrealized deeds to be reconciled between law and morals in this world, for their ongoing volatile righteous battles, of which I consider myself a suspect, by biased deeds of judgment, intolerances, discrimination, and fleshly vanities, of which law ineffectively fails to apply a moral code, short of the love shown in laws' of its closest interpretation in Jesus Christ. Hoping for a continued grace under the blood of Jesus Christ, I believe justice is working by a greater power that governs our lives now than by that which was justifiable only through the law, most prevalent prior to Christ's resurrection. The power of the Holy Spirit moves to faith the hearts and minds of people to obey God's laws. By faith, another mistrial of Jesus Christ by a self-righteous elite society is unlikely to be repeated without God's justice. By timely execution of events, and in worst case scenario, at the second return of His Son to rule the world, justice will be served by the One Whom God Has given all authority: Jesus Christ.

XV. Truth

*"I have no greater joy than to hear that my children walk
in truth."*
(3 John 1:4)

> We seek higher truths in Godly judgments when
> troubles and conflicts arise, seeking the precepts
> of perfection in face of our rebellions. Lawless,
> some roam without a God.

I AM THE SON of God; I look like him in body and Spirit. We share
similar features; for the fig tree doesn't bear olives, nor can darkness beget light (1 John 1:5). The sun always rises from the east and
sets in the west—a self-evident truth—upon which life has sprung
by rain brought in by clouds to the green pastures and mountains,
to form the seas and rivers of life-giving waters, sustaining all living creatures. By such witness to nature is our common experience to truth about ourselves and others; by association of our
similarities and differences, by distinguishing between rights and
wrongs—righteousness and sin. Upholding our rights in life as
immutable, we sought truths undeterred by relative experiences
of life, more grounded in an absolute path to life. Unhindered by
our differences from others, absolute truth required a reason of
faith in the unseen, by evidence of much greater magnitude in its
absence. The infinite realm, outside our comprehension, with its
closest representation in the abstraction of our dreams, awake we
seek higher truths in reality by an unwavering Godly judgment to

anchor reality, stirring our rebellious self out of sleep. Not always in line with our sense of logic, truth establishes the foundation upon which we live, in spite of its far-fetched disbelief: Sarai's dismissal of the childbearing prophecy to Abraham by God (Genesis 18:12), the doubtful adoption of the long journey before Jacob on the promised ladder to heaven (Genesis 28), or the massacre of innocent infants by Herod in denial of the acceptance of the sovereignty of the new born baby Jesus. Falsely, some roam without a God; belligerent, we inflict death, like Cain, whose deeds lacked any other truths outside of his own temporal impulses, by which generations were born to terms with, debilitating truths about covetous acts.

Few who adopted the words of God were moved by its power: *"For the word of God is living and powerful, and sharper than any two-edged sword, piercing even to the division of soul and spirit, and joints and marrow, and is a discerner of the thoughts and intents of the heart." (Hebrews 4:12)*. More exaggerated were ambitions to erect a less comprehensive man-made laws to gods with no basis of truth, in which the more ordained tabloid of stones was set aside, in spite of their ordinance to establish an absolute truth about God, having derailed roadways to the floods of evils done by a nation seeking to reach the seat of God by inadequate heights of an incomplete tower to knowledge. Absolute evidence of truths about God's omnipresence and omnipotence is revealed in Christ, whom God sends to represent the truths of His word. In His outrage, God searched for those whom truths may not be watered down by its superlatives—or derivatives—of an incomplete account to truths, diverting efforts to draw near to God by catastrophic pleas of mercy. The strayed kings: Rehoboam, Abijam, Jehoram, Ahaziah, Athaliah, Ahaz, Manasseh, Zedekiah, and many others, who turned away from the truth, replacing God by some other contrived, made-up idols and images, causing reversal of His earlier blessings to Israel.

> *Lacking absolutes, multiplicities of truths have emerged requiring a probabilistic inclusion of the "maybe".*

Recurring drifts to idol worship necessitated a more permanent solution to a wandering man seeking reasonable living. To God, the immortality to life is arguably soberer in its ambition to achievement of perfection than the sullied strife of mortals, with hurried, rash aspirations unto death. Life required a less morally challenged man, more to the likeness of God, anointed by His Spirit, in the flesh, making a sacrifice to the purposes of justice by a slacking truth of hand-made carved images. Requiring a sacrifice without a blemish, God would immaculately conceive Jesus to become the sinless perfection of truth, delivering a message to the world as evidence to God's sovereignty and power: *"You are a king, then!" said Pilate. Jesus answered, "You say that I am a king. In fact, the reason I was born and came into the world is to testify to the truth. Everyone on the side of truth listens to me." (John 18:37-38).*

Amending loopholes to all rebellious acts of man against the law are supplemented with a collateral bail to an impending verdict of death to the King of the Jews, who has challenged their truth about their understanding of the law by which they've arrested Him. Claiming to be *"the truth, the way, and the life"*, Jesus death had no imminent ramifications, for if it did, truth about His resurrection would make all believe in Jesus Christ. But many have devised anti-truth, as a disregard for the evidences of Jesus' life and death. The absolute truth of Jesus' compassion and love have been thwarted under a false, deceiving ideal of coexistence, that has proven ineffective by world affairs, masking His imminent return to Judge by a less drastic call to repent.

Lacking absolutes, multiplicities of truths have emerged requiring a probabilistic inclusion of the "maybes", which in spite of their prevalence, give an absurd assurance about the future, without guarantees, risking a crucial binary decision, of life or death magnitude, misleading ourselves and others. Why we remain aloof to the truth of Jesus Christ deity is controversial. Similarly risky is the disregard of the divinity of Jesus as the Son of God, which by exclusion, a great subject of philosophical argument is eroded from the domains of the material world, stagnating the institution of faith behind the confluences of the laissez-faire. I, on the other hand, was convicted by Jesus' elegant proof to the paralytic, when He backed up His truthful claims to forgiveness by raising Him from His bed: *"which is easier to say to the paralytic "your sins are forgiven, or to say, "Arise take up your bed and walk." But that you may know that the Son of Man has power on earth to forgive sin— He said to the paralytic, "I say to you, arise, take up your bed and go to your house." (Mark 2:9-11).*

XVI. Faith

"That the sharing of your faith may become effective by
the acknowledgement of every good thing which is in you
in Christ Jesus."
(Philemon 1:6)

> *astrological signs . . . tying our curiosities about*
> *our futures intimately with our love affairs, in*
> *an overwhelming popularity without any guar-*
> *antees or reliability*

IN RECENT YEARS ONLINE dating has become increasingly popular
in response to the needed convenience by many pressed for time
to have a meaningful relationship or meet a partner. The plethora
of online applications catering to these individuals is indicative of
what they have termed "recession proof businesses", a testimony to
the sustained demands and the range of services these businesses
provide to the much needed commodity of "love". Fascinated by
the concept, I have dedicated a considerable amount of time to discover the dynamics of such a paradigm. I opened several accounts
on some online websites, creating a profile in which I attempted a
detailed description of myself with some of my best photographs,
some textual description about what I do, and the type of person
I'm looking for. Thanks to the ease by which these websites are
designed, user profile creation has become increasingly easier to
attract more users through a simple user-friendly interfaces, using
"toggle" buttons to enable features that allow for unique virtual

presence, some with exotic images complementing users' profiles. I recall spending hours browsing through hundreds of profile pictures, reading through many graphic details, conveniently delivered to my monitor, exceedingly excited about the prospects of a real connection to one of these virtual figures. When the websites' recommended prospects did not match my preferences, I would use keywords in search functions to return more users with more graphic details. There was no right or wrong way to do a search; a pictorially appeasing result always indicated a desirably successful search. I, like many others, was disinterested in profiles without images, investing more time and effort in assessing users who had multiple descriptive pictures, at times disregarding usual built-in matching functionality intended to automatically pair users according to preferences. The big test was always in the pudding; if and when an online connection resulted in a face-to-face meeting in which the online profile description validated the mental image one had of their match, or more often than not, irrevocably negated it. In positive outcomes, where the image matched the description, a lurking doubt about other profile matches always hanged in the distance, while negative outcomes only resulted in more time consuming searches.

The disappointing outcomes of these meetings surprisingly didn't always seem to slow-down or stop people from their online activities and accounts. Many, myself included, went back to reattempt their search criteria until some desirable results were achieved. In response to demands, and enhancing their online search matching algorithms, some websites boosted their search engines with the infamous predictability of astrological sign matching criteria, linking partners to websites they've collaborated and marketed with, tying our curiosities about our futures intimately with our love affairs, in an overwhelming popularity without any guarantees or reliability.

These businesses are more active and profitable than many other viable businesses on the internet, speaking volumes to our character preferences. Volatile, we have become increasingly image-dependent that our stimulation response is seen by the magnitude we have consecrated an entire online paradigm, almost exclusively based on images without which it would be unapproachable. Some augmented with hypothetical images, our evolving visual bias readily disregards much of what's not obvious or clearly visible, conforming more easily to what we can see and feel. Less conducive to a response were profiles without pictures. Even more difficult a concept, requiring a greater leap of faith, is the act of going on a "blind date" with a person whose profile has no real image and a consistent astrological forecast pointing to doomsday.

> *Requiring a greater leap of faith is the act of going on a "blind date" with a person whose profile has no real image and a consistent astrological forecast pointing to doomsday.*

Likewise, a date with Jesus' many find too abstract to grasp, requiring much faith in an imageless God, that only few have ventured by faith to experience. Betting closer relationships on visible altars, we prefer a match by a much simpler toggle interface before a complex algorithm to an unknown future. By the experiences of others, we gain a greater sense of security over the less image-based word of God, requiring a more arduous exercise of faith: "*Now faith is the substance of things hoped for, the evidence of things not seen. For by it the elders obtained a good testimony. By faith we understand that the worlds are framed by the word of God, so that the things which are seen were not made of things which are visible.*" (Hebrews 11:1-3).

Rewarding was Jesus' profile promise to those who subscribed to it when He said: "*All that the Father gives Me will come to Me, and the one who comes to me I will by no means cast out.*" (John 6:37). Some have struggled with faith, requiring more proof, like Thomas, Jesus' disciple, who insisted to see Jesus' nail scars to believe, to whom Jesus' appearance compelled to faith: "*Thomas, because you have seen Me, you have believed. Blessed are those who have not seen and yet have believed.*" (John 20:29). Although Jesus had not turned away any that have waited on Him, how God determines His chosen remains largely to His discretion. For others, however; a mustard-size seed of faith is said to have moved mountains: *"He replied, "Because you have so little faith. Truly, I tell you, if you have faith as small as a mustard seed, you can say to this mountain, "Move from here to there," and it will move. Nothing will be impossible for you."" (Matthew 17:20).*

XVII. Joy

"My brethren, count it all joy when you fall into various trials, knowing that the testing of your faith produces patience."
(James 1:2)

> *Having the mind of Christ over matters, our joy is multiplied by overcoming the limitations that persistently seek to define us when we do not have the power of Christ and His Holy Spirit.*

"SILVER AND GOLD *I do not have, but what I do have I give you; in the name of Jesus Christ of Nazareth, rise up and walk." (Acts 3:4)* was Peter's command to the lame-since-birth man who rose from the temple gates where he was begging. He leapt for joy inside the temple, whom few minutes' prior couldn't walk. Causing many with him to be similarly joyful, the lame man's faith and prudence were a testimony to his leaping feet. It may have required long years of suffering before the moment of joy this man had truly lived and felt; perhaps most momentous joy which he had never before experienced. Having the mind of Christ over matters, our joys are multiplied when by faith we overcome the limitations of our flesh: *"for who knows the mind of God, but we have the mind of Christ"*. Many times measured in terms of our pains, the source of triumphant joy requires continuous diligence in the promises of God to the grace and mercies He delivers to those who seek Him. Empowered by the faith of Peter, God healed the lame man's legs, causing great joy to him and everyone else who witnessed the miracle.

But joy is hard to attain when death is hanging in the balance. Unlike the lame man's terminal joy when he regained his walking feet, Jesus' life on earth commemorated a terminal death to which He knew to be His verdict by a multitude who had no hesitation to deny Him publicly. With an overestimated zeal, many like Jesus' closest disciple Peter, who offered to be crucified in His place (Mark 8:33), would deny Him at Herod's courts. Unbelieving, doubt took over the joy they've experienced during their life with Jesus, that in spite of the miracles that they witnessed they retreated in fear before His arrest and crucifixion. Influenced by the very meaning of power He had come to change, many joys were overshadowed in light of the cross of Jesus, before He would complete the mission He had been set out to accomplish. Overcoming death, the last enemy of mankind, Jesus would rise to change our destiny from the morbidity of mortality to the joy of resurrection. Moreover, Jesus would also change the minds and hearts of those who believe in Him, no longer with doubt, they would be given the minds of Christ and His Holy Spirit to change their own definition of joy that validated the model they have witnessed in Jesus during His life on earth.

Transcending earthly joy, Jesus' monumental moments of joy were anointed by the Holy Spirit such as those of baptism by John the Baptist and during transfiguration on the mountain with Elijah and Abraham. Jesus' inspired many who discovered spiritual joy in a world which absurdly lacks it. Becoming the corner stone to what later became His church, Jesus' life changed many others' whose lives have been dull prior to meeting Him. Living on disposed pieces of false hope, like the lame man at the temple gates, contiguously enduring through decades of time in pursuit of a miracle, before a break through to his feeble knees joyously affirmed his faith: *"therefore strengthen the hands which hang down, and the feeble knees, and make straight paths for your feet, so that what is lame may not be dislocated, but rather be healed" (Hebrews 12:12-13).* Beginning with our first steps to the discovery of joy, to the marathons of inquisitions garnishing our aspiration to divine fulfillment, our moments of happiness are fleeting to an irreversible time. Joy is always in strife; rarely present in the now. There is always somewhere else we would rather be, another person we aspire to be like, something else we wish to have. We are thrilled by the occasional treat to a free gift that revives our senses of worth; the joys of feeling accepted and loved, most often felt when we are filled by the Holy Spirit through Christ Jesus. The tutor of our faith, Jesus became the conveyor by which we obtained a much autonomous relationship with God where in our pursuit of His kingdom our means to joy are changed in light of His salvation: "*the joy of the Lord is our strength.*" *(Nehemiah 8:10).*

> *Comparable to moments of love at first sight, their encounter with Jesus must have been so joyful that it implored them to leave all and follow Him.*

Proving futile the reliance on others, Jesus' encounters are transformational, doing away with the anxieties of life by the joys of a promise to another life, that the fishermen left their pursuit of their oats in fish, and followed Him who filled their nets to the full. Soon their lives would change from the mundane labor of fishing to an extraordinary reality to which they would dedicate their entire lives to. Comparable to moments of love at first sight, their encounter with Jesus must have been so joyful that it implored them to leave all and follow Him. Their lives became a history of euphoric miracles: walking on water, raising the dead, giving sight to the blind, hearing to the deaf, speech to the mute, healing the bleeding wounds, and the occasional anointing by very expensive spikenard to the head and feet of Jesus. Like the parable of the precious pearl, so is Christ's joy in its attainment: worth everything. Likewise, much joy God derives from His creation, that nothing less of His Son Jesus Christ would suffice for Him to redeem us: "*For God so loved the world, that He gave His only begotten Son, that whomever believes in Him shall not perish, but have eternal life." (John 3:16).*

Narrow is the way, however; that leads to eternal salvation. Found in Jesus Christ, the joy of God, His only begotten Son, whom God ordained before time, endured the chastening of faith during times of tribulation. Like the lame man, whose great joy was the result of his prudent faith, so was Christ's prudence in suffering to entitle us to the eternal joy of salvation, to be called the sons of God: "*strengthened with all might, according to His glorious power, for all patience and longsuffering with joy; giving thanks to the Father who has qualified us to be partakers of the inheritance of the saints in the light*" (*Colossians 1:11*). Preparing our worth to His kingdom, Christ became the joy of those whom in suffering were faithful to Him: "*Well done, good and faithful servant; you were faithful over a few things, I will make you ruler over many things. Enter into the joy of your lord." (Matthew 25:21).*

Jesus' life made joyful those around Him. His visionary leadership restored our sights to things not seen by the eyes of the world. The exuberant resurrection following His brief burial would convict Christians for generations to come, and alleviate the difficult transition to a world without Him, compelling them to carry His message and their testimonies to the ends of the earth (Mark 16:15), living joyously in the brief years of life, while recognizing that most joyous moments were never in the things attained, but through the assurance and revelation of Jesus Christ by the Holy Spirit in their lives.

XVIII. Righteousness

"Judge not, and you shall not be judged. Condemn not,
and you shall not be condemned. Forgive, and you will be
forgiven. Give and it will be given to you: good measure,
pressed down, shaken together, and running over will be
put in your bosoms. For with the same measure you use,
it will be measured back to you."
(Luke 6:37-38)

> *Righteousness, synonymous with many boast-*
> *ful meanings, wrongfully inspired many to the*
> *more accepted norms of the self-affirming ma-*
> *jority of law keepers.*

To PILATE, JESUS' ARRIVAL in his courts for trial over tax eva-
sion to Caesar was not entirely out-of-character to the seemingly
abrupt reputation he had conjured of Jesus as disruptive person,
with a persona that takes matters too seriously on himself and
others (Luke 23:2). Uncouth in his methods of inquisition with a
shrewd and uncanny determination, Pilate questions Jesus, reit-
eratively unbelieving of His defamed miracles on a mask of misfits
who followed Him as the Son of God, who were unsettled by the
havoc they created to the multitudes who believed Jesus to be the
Messiah. Pilate's agitated discomfort and lack of self-confidence in
placing judgment made an implicitly annulled pardon a remorse-
ful exit of Jesus, claiming His innocence, and sending Him to a trial
in Herod's court. Herod's judgement was finalized when, through

betrayal of Jesus' close disciple Judas, the crowd perturbs the silent courts of Herod pleading for Barnabas' release. To many, Jesus' arrest was an awaited relief from a figure whose righteous acts were perceived arrogantly as blown-up behavior worthy of lawful death, bartering the forgiveness of the released criminal Barnabas over the miraculous works of Jesus. They stripped Jesus of His garment and robed Him in sackcloth of shame, as if unthreading a divine plan meshed by a bribed oath of a deteriorating law Jesus had previously predicted to them, to which He had the pejorative to rectify.

Out of obligation and decorum, Herod's trial yielded the desired outcome for His court dignitaries and the people by releasing an alleged criminal by arresting a righteous man. Where Pilate found no fault of unlawful acts, the righteousness of Jesus' life unveiled the horrific populace mediocrity cloaked in righteous acts through the law. Righteousness, synonymous with many boastful meanings, wrongfully inspired many to the more accepted norms of the self-affirming majority of law keepers, who were moved to judgment by an incomplete account of evidence. Pharisees and Sadducees were often righteous, they maintained strict religious rituals that they had adhered to primarily by an inspiration of differences that have set them on a higher ground from others. Derived from desire to do the "right thing", righteousness inspired through them was bounded by the limitation of their humanness and the sustained demands of their status quo adherences, scantly steering them off off their traditions to reach the full measure of righteousness—almost always—skewed by the public majority. Jesus was completely innocent of any crime when they brought Him to Pilates and Herod, those who out of self-righteousness strongly believed their moral superiority. Lost in the populace coherence to their righteous virtue, the crowds pleaded to kill an innocent man by what they've perceived as a righteous act, disregarding any conscious evidence to the contrary. Where it is not sought, such limited self-righteousness, exhibited and supported by Jesus' prosecutors, present boundaries which are not always comforted by comparison to the measures of righteousness by law which challenges their moral rigor to place judgment on others.

> *righteousness by law cast the nail in Jesus' coffin, whose righteousness far exceeded those whom by law, executed Him on the cross.*

While all righteousness finds its root in a "god", our deep desire to please combined with our imperfections in presenting a "more perfect" sacrifice, had justified the means to a righteous judgment. Jesus' trials were ideal example of such truth, where a greater achievement to righteousness blinded the eyes of justice to the process by which they would sentence an innocent man to the cross, for liberally challenging their ceremonial rituals, like those of the Sabbath keeping, replacing them by unorthodox teachings about love. Keeping with their Sabbaths customs which they held with similar zeal to the practices of circumcision of the Law of Moses, the overarching righteousness to Jesus' liberality and compassion to heal the sick, seeking mercy over sacrifice, is overlooked: *"Jesus answered and said to them, "I did one work, and you marvel. Moses therefore gave you circumcision (not that it is from Moses, but from the fathers), and you circumcise a man on the Sabbath. If a man receives circumcision on the Sabbath so that the law of Moses should not be broken, are you angry with Me because I made a man completely well on the Sabbath?" (John 7:21-23).* The explicit "dos" and "don'ts" of the law won over the more implicit aspiration of mercy, often characterizing the Good Samaritans, by whom a greater compassion to save a stranger's life is valued as less righteous in the eyes of some with more virtuous judgement of a law against trespassers. Less compelled to extend a helping hand to a suffering man, godly priests and Levites find their righteousness contained in the keeping of the law (Luke 10:30-37). Proving to lead to spiritual stagnation and death, righteousness by law cast the nail in Jesus' coffin, whose righteousness far exceeded those whom by law, executed Him on the cross.

XVIII. Righteousness

Done out of deep convictions, lawful works rarely justify intents or deeds, for many brotherly deeds are done out of care and loyalty to others, uniting in atrocious causes of lawful violence. Righteous actions, however; are rarely from a source of disbelief. By strong faith, righteousness is given relevance—a spirit to the law—by which God planned to show His mercies towards man. Abolishing the letter of the law, Jesus died to the law by a self-sacrifice to the magnitude of a temporary abolishment of God, to redeem His followers who have been confined under the verdict of death by the law in which all have sinned: *"But now the righteousness of God apart from the law is revealed, being witnessed by the Law and the Prophets, even the righteousness of God, through faith in Jesus Christ, to all and on all who believe. For there is no difference; for all have sinned and fall short of the glory of God." (Romans 3:21-22).* In light of the character of the Good Samaritan, a righteousness parable is demonstrated to strangers in Jesus Christ, whose righteousness fulfills the scripture of the law by its spirit of love to all who believe: *"But the scripture has confined all under sin, that the promise of faith in Jesus Christ might be given to those who believe." (Galatians 3:22).*

Jesus' journey to the cross diminished the inseparable evil of our nature from the path of unrighteousness leading to death: *"In the way of righteousness is life, and its pathway there is no death" (Proverbs 12:18).* Unlike the path of unrighteousness, righteousness thrives in light of Christ's faith-driven acts by which unrighteousness vanishes. Thriving on thoughts and deeds, shadows of unrighteousness do not hold virtue by the mere reality of their esoteric nature, lacking definition, detracting life from its destination. Deceptive in its imitation, misleading shadows have crossed paths with shadows of others that have given way to darkness, standing in light of truth. Shadows did not diminish the light of Jesus Christ in spite of the doubt they cast on an otherwise nonnegotiable truth regarding His Godliness. It is critical, therefore, to distinguish between random, uninspired acts of righteousness versus those of righteousness-by-faith in Jesus Christ (Philippians 3:8-9), where faith and action are a direct result of the influence of the Holy Spirit, inspired by evidence of life in Jesus Christ. Justified by the sacrificial death of Jesus to the law, a more excellent path of perfect righteousness in Christ is established, to shine away our shadows of death, without blemish or excuse, standing firm by the gift of the Holy Spirit before the judgment of God: "*And if Christ is in you, the body is dead because of sin, but the Spirit is life because of righteousness. But if the Spirit of Him who raised Jesus from the dead dwells in you, He who raised Christ from the dead will also give life to your mortal bodies through His Spirit who dwells in you.*" *(Romans 8:10).*

Having withstood His mistrials, Jesus shall return to judge an unrighteous world that have perverted the truth about His life and His resurrection. Meanwhile, we live not by a contrived act of righteousness, but by an inspired discernment to righteousness of the Holy Spirit: "*So that you may be able to discern what is best and may be pure and blameless for the day of Christ, filled with the fruit of righteousness that comes through Jesus Christ—to the glory and praise of God.*" *(Philippians 1:10-11).*

XIX. Holy Spirit

"But the hour is coming, and is now here, when the true worshipers will worship the Father in spirit and truth, for the Father is seeking such people to worship Him. God is spirit, and those who worship Him must worship in spirit and truth."
(John 4:23-24)

> *The Holy Spirit is the agent who moves us through prayers to experience God, not by what we know, but rather, by what is revealed*

GOD IS A SPIRIT with no set shape or form. Like energy, for lack of a better comparison, God's Spirit is not seen in spite of its often felt essence which is similar to those of light and heat. The difficulty in defining the Spirit of God by an image baffled some who find the concept of God too abstruse to grasp without God's spiritual representation embodied in Jesus Christ. Similar energy generated from the Spirit of God was the agent that evoked the world into creation. God's voice perturbations caused the material world to form by God's words, which vibrated matter into Spirit encapsulated life. In a way, we live in a world that floats in God's Spirit, through whom we move and breathe: *"For in Him we live and move and have our beings." (Acts 17:28)*. Vibrating with energy, we are God's instrument that connect our spirit to God. Encompassing our awareness and consciousness is our link to God through His Holy Spirit: *"There is one body and one Spirit, just as you were called to one hope when you were called; one Lord, one faith, one baptism; one God and Father of all, who is over all and through all and in all"* (Ephesians 4:4). Extrapolating on this truth signifies our communication with God's Holy Spirit who attunes our souls to Him in this energy vibrating universe, transcending our means of understanding Him in relationship to ourselves and to others. Created for His pleasure *"Praise be to the God and Father of our Lord Jesus Christ, who has blessed us in the heavenly realms with every spiritual blessing in Christ. For He chose us in him before the creation of the world to be holy and blameless in his sight. In love He predestined us for adoption to sonship through Jesus Christ, in accordance with His pleasure and will – to the praise of His glorious grace, which He has freely given us in the One He loves." (Ephesians 1:3-5)*, our pulsating lives brings us to experience the joy of God in a new light, in which His Holy Spirit reveals itself, unbound by the means of the physical world. The Holy Spirit is the agent who moves us through prayers to experience God, not by what we know, but rather, by what is revealed: *"For whom among men knows the thoughts of a man except the man's spirit within him? In the same way no-one knows the thoughts of God except in the Spirit." (1 Corinthians 2:11)*.

God's words are the inspired physical evidence of the Holy Spirit which we acquired by revelation and knowledge and used to plea to attain to the spiritual righteousness and Godly favor. Through our spirit we strive to become the spiritual Godly character necessary for our spiritual survival. Elevated from the less spiritual elements of the flesh in which our bodily temples suffer to death, we constructively maintain a spiritual outlook to sustain our lives by the word of God surpassing innate desire by the elements of the flesh to replacement by the more Spiritual elements of Jesus Christ. Those spiritual qualities pertaining to *faith, hope, love, joy, peace, longsuffering, kindness, goodness, faithfulness, gentleness, and self-control (Galatians 5:22)*, over the fleshly qualities of *wrath, sorcery, adultery, and fornications (Galatians 5:24)*. When exhibited, spiritual traits clearly reflect on unique characteristics

that distinguish those who have attained the knowledge and fulfillment of the Holy Spirit of God from those who have not.

> *Spiritual growth is the discernment and knowl-
> edge of the Spirit of God, preparing our flesh
> to be the vessel through which the Holy Spirit
> moves with powerful manifestations.*

Therefore, God, His word, and the Holy Spirit, are equally
interchangeable, representative of the one entity of God, converg-
ing to a man in Jesus Christ, who created everything, through Him
everything came into being, including His immaculate conception
into the physical world by the transcending of the Holy Spirit on
the virgin Mary, becoming God's appearance in the flesh: "*And the
Word became flesh and dwelt among us, and we beheld His glory,
the glory as the only begotten of the Father, full of grace and truth.*"
(*John 1:14*). Prior, God used clouds, pillars of light, and signs of
nature—and more effectively—people, to communicate His word
to us, before a more pervasive method of communication was
deemed necessary to an ever rebellious nation distracted by the
growing demands of the elements of the flesh. Hoping to achieve a
more desirable inspiration to life than the fate of death, God sends
His Holy Spirit to all those who would follow the example of His
Son Jesus Christ. Our faith in Christ builds our spiritual muscles
by the blood of His sacrifice given through the Holy Spirit, delivering much needed sustenance to our spiritual beings, otherwise
unquenched by earthly means. Spiritual growth is the discernment
and knowledge of the Spirit of God, preparing our flesh to be the
vessels through which the Holy Spirit moves with powerful manifestation to all facets of our lives, where the miracle of life abounds.

Giving much evidence to the living word of God, Jesus's power
of the Holy Spirit repeatedly alleviated much of the ailing flesh by
example to those whom He taught, as well as, those who followed
Him. An embodiment to God's word, Jesus became the fulfillment
of time in the spirit inspired prophecies, predicted since creation.

By Jesus' final ascension to heaven, the evident workmanship of the trinity of God, Jesus Christ and the Holy Spirit was given truth, overcoming death, to all those who believe and witness to Jesus Christ as their Lord and Savior. Fulfilling Jesus' promises, the Holy Spirit descended on His disciples in tongues of fire (Acts 2:3) after Jesus' resurrection, to deliver on God's word and promise to send the "comforter": *"And I will pray the Father and He will give you another comforter, to be with you forever, the Spirit of truth."* *(John 14:15).* The Holy Spirit became the invisible spiritual guide, working through us to do the will of God until the end of times: *"Behold, I send the Promise of My Father upon you; but tarry in the city of Jerusalem until you are endued with power from on high."* *(Luke 24:49).*

It is through the Holy Spirit that God moves His most powerful vice against all powers and principalities of this world to reveal the mysteries of His divine plan for our lives. In our bowed hearts before God's word, the powerful gift of the Holy Spirit transforms our lives by that which began and finished in Jesus Christ.

XX. Absolute

"I am the Alpha and the Omega, the beginning and the End," says the Lord, "who is and who was and who is to come, the Almighty."
(Revelation 1:8)

> *Vision after eating the fruit, implies a new dimension of perception...a more relative insight into a deeper self in which a feeling or perception of "nakedness" is experienced.*

IS IT POSSIBLE TO understand the good without the bad, love without hate, grace without shame, faith without doubt, light without darkness, or God without Satan? In our search of the absolute—the invariable unity of an unequivocal state of being God—one stumbles on the relative, to fathom unreachable limits that defy purpose. Short of a definitive beginning, the diminishing distance to the knowledge of the absolute perfect God, appears further away from our understanding, with no end in sight. It draws us in by desire to a tree of knowledge in which a man's Godly aspirations to absolute perfection reverts his life to death, having overlooked an absolute instruction to a prohibited boundary.

While the fall of man in the story of creation have triggered many interpretations about absolute virtues, one striking feature of the story is the definitive relativism of "vision" experienced by Eve before and after eating from the tree of knowledge: *"So when the woman saw that the tree was good for food, that it was pleasant to the eyes, and a tree desirable to make one wise, she took of its fruit and ate. She also gave to her husband with her, and he ate. Then the eyes of both of them were opened." (Genesis 3:6 -7).* Vision after eating the fruit implies a new dimension of perception than prior: the former is the absolute explicitness of seeing without perceiving, the latter is a more relative insight into a deeper self in which a feeling or perception of "nakedness" is experienced, as indicated in *(Genesis 3:7) "and they knew that they were naked."* Implied an intake of something external, or outside of the self, the act of "eating" represented by the tree of knowledge modified the state of Adam and Eve's vision, adding a dimension, perhaps a diffusive immersion, causing a reconfiguration of the self, an alteration of the mind and soul, most likened to a possessed state where one senses a different reality they had no prior knowledge of, by which they were transformed. The agent serpent most likely acquired a similar state by similar means of ingestion that morphed it into a forbidden awareness.

It may be readily interpreted that virtues, whether good or evil, like the fruit of the tree, are discrete entities capable of embodiment by an act of willful procurement, the putting on of robes of righteousness or unrighteousness, which when worn, our souls are transformed accordingly. Requiring more perception, virtues and anti-virtues evolved our understanding from the mere explicitness of acts without knowledge of virtues; the no-virtue, or rather the indifferent ignorance of the difference between right and wrong, righteousness and sin. While "knowledge" added an awareness to senses that were otherwise not within the realm of consciousness, the encounter with the serpent provided no use or application to knowledge apart from distinguishing between their current state and the absolute righteousness which they had previously possessed.

It is also possible that Adam and Eve were the inert, unrealized expression of virtues. Pending enactment, they exercised absolutely good virtue until the time when their anti-virtues were enabled by eating from the tree of knowledge. The act of eating of the fruit is only symbolic to the awakening of the senses from a preexisting state of awareness of the mind by which a desire to a known vice is brought to consciousness. Differing from the possessive act of anti-virtue demonstrated by intake of the fruit, enablement of preexisting virtues places all elements of virtuous and non-virtuous qualities inside of man—not as discrete external qualities—with a necessary enabler such as that of the forbidden fruit.

> Hence the forbidden "tree of knowledge" can be also interpreted as "the tree of ignorance" given the relative tacit knowledge it initiated, by which man only learned about their inadequacies.

Awareness gained by expression of unrealized anti-virtues would prove similarly futile in its dispensation of sin to awareness by possession, leading to a purposeless end, when both are a consequence of breaking an absolute law. The significance of purpose to knowledge is readily understood by comparison of the acts of infants to those of adults, where intents and deeds weigh in on the differentiator between a virtue and vice. Actions, whether good or bad, are only relative matters with respect to awareness; deeds, on the other hand, differentiate between virtue and anti-virtue. Where actions are more an intent in adults leading to immorality, not much judgment is given to infants and children whose actions lack any cohesive moral or virtuous intent. Absolute enablement of virtue and non-virtue compete against one another in our minds, where enactment is a matter of purposeful intent and deed, most evident battles between the flesh and the spirit take their root inside of man: "*For the flesh lusts against the Spirit, and the Spirit against the flesh; and they are contrary to one another, so that you do not do the things that you wish." (Galatians 5:17)*.

Since by definition of absolutes no relatives are found, for ignorance cannot be found in knowledge, just as there is no evil in goodness, it can be inferred that Adam and Eve were created with the absolute virtues of God without anti-virtue. Adam's sin dispossessed the distilled confluences of all absolute Godly virtues by knowledge of the relative anti-virtue, or what became known as sin. Hence the forbidden "tree of knowledge" can be also interpreted as "the tree of ignorance" given the relative tacit knowledge it initiated, by which man only learned about their inadequacies. While it had "puffed up" their perception, neither the serpent nor Adam and Eve knew what to make of their new awareness except for the absolute punishment to which they've became destined.

Relative life replaced the more absolute virtuous life through survival-by-labor to which man was sentenced, leading the way for many subsequent generations that would follow in the same path. Born with dispossessed virtues, man either had an innate call to an absolute life, or a lukewarm indifference by a suitable contentment with its relative. Seeking absolute dominance and control over life man struggled to achieve absolute peace and coherence to sustain their relative knowledge without consistently deferring to an unbiased intervention by a moderator, to whom perfection has been attributed, perceptively and explicitly, in the undefinable, absolute being of God.

> *Jesus' resurrection defiled death—the last enemy of man—whom God puts to absolute rest for those enacting from a place of an imperfectly relative faith.*

A much needed resolution to the imperfect dynamics of matters relating to life and death began to incur a cost on the more absolute life seekers, who, distant from Adam, sought better consequences to judgments from others and God. Neither the dispossession of evil spirits of demon-possessed men, nor the healing of the leprous skin, could the miracles of Jesus prove to restore absolute perfection, except in the one who performed them. The only remedy to man's anti-virtue was anecdotal to the same perceptive quality of vision Adam and Eve had acquired when they ate of the fruit, the central quality of faith: *"Now faith is the substance*

of things hoped for, the evidence of things not seen." (Hebrews 11:1).
In the example of the one absolute personification of God in Jesus
Christ, faith afforded mankind's return to absolute virtues away
from the ill choices that started with Adam. Jesus inspires our lives
to a better stature in the infinite knowledge of God, by which we
may purpose life, by faith, in an absolute embodiment of perfection, either putting on Christ's perfect robes of virtues or by the
shedding of an engrained being of an imperfect man, to an image
of God's likeness, achieving a new meaning to an absolute life, un-
adulterated by death.

By an absolute reversal of the imperfections of Adam, God's
love is repurposed in the sacrificial death of a new Adam—Jesus
Christ—bridging the distance between an absolute God and a relative man. Through Jesus Christ, God's definitions of an absolute
free gift of grace is achieved to remediate an unachievable absolute
law that sentenced man to a relative life—or death—by ignorance
to knowledge. Reserving the rights to an absolute act of life, Jesus'
resurrection defiled death—the last enemy of man—whom God
puts to absolute rest for those enacting from a place of an imper-
fectly relative faith.

*Jesus answered, "I am the way and the truth and the life. No
one comes to the Father except through me." John 14:6*

XXI. Jesus Christ

"And Jesus came and spoke unto them, saying, "All power
is given unto me in heaven and in earth."
(Matthew 28:18)

> *Jesus' most difficult task was being the spiri-*
> *tual man of God, in whose image we have all*
> *been created, to a law-driven nation that have*
> *struggled to see outside of the present.*

LOVE HAS NEVER KNOWN a greater meaning than by that which
was revealed in Jesus Christ. Few claimed such a fervent love towards the Lord, like John, who laid his head on the heart of Jesus,
and Martha, who poured an expensive spikenard on Jesus' feet,
much like the tearful woman who wiped Jesus' feet with her hair.
Jesus captured the hearts of many who met Him, who found a connection with Him on a personal level, unequivocal to any other
connection they've experienced. Jesus was more than the love
people felt towards Him, however. Jesus was a man with a critical
mission on earth that He was set out to accomplish, that having
the pre-knowledge to time burdened Him with the lives and souls
of those whom He met. Jesus' most difficult task was being the
spiritual man of God in whose image we have all been created, to a
law-driven nation that have struggled to see outside of the present.
Visions of descending doves and angels paved the path to Jesus'
arrival to the witnesses who would—out of love—foretell His
stories of the nativity leading to His ascension and beyond. Most

influential in world History, Jesus' become the man most desirable by generations preparing to to meet Him and await His return to take them to heaven. When on earth, people thronged to touch Him—any part of Him—in faith that their bleeding calamities and illnesses will depart, Jesus sought after the twelve few, whom He would call the light of the world, the salt without which sustenance would lose its taste. Jesus' strength emanated from a strong spiritual being that overcame the trials of Satan, sustaining forty days of fasting in a wilderness on His own, while blessing the thousands with baskets full of bread. *"In remembrance of Me"*, Jesus said to His disciples, when He broke the bread and drank the wine in the Passover feast before He would be crucified, setting the Eucharist as the symbol by which we would recall all the miracles of His time on earth and the power of His resurrection. Given all Godly power, Jesus challenged those who relied on their strengths, that their blasphemous accusations against Him didn't stand in spite of the ultimate punishment of His death on the cross, when He arose victoriously to reunite with those to whom He reappeared. Predicted since man knew time, an affair with Jesus' became the obvious choice to many whose testimonies are a mind boggling unity, out of an intuitive conviction which defies worldly logic, pointing to a deeper connection with someone much greater than themselves. In spite of all evidences to Jesus' life on earth and His divinity, many who loved Him cared less about a proof in the face of the love they felt for Him, while some, putting their hands to the plow, gave all they had to follow Him, never looking back. Humbly Jesus came to the world to glorify a scene of a manger that would inspire meekness to kings and kingdoms to follow. Riding on a colt to Jerusalem, Jesus' promised city would be riding on the clouds, transcending before the eyes of those who would find it difficult to stand before the exuberance of His divinity. An early teacher, Jesus would provoke those who rushed to stone Him on account of His claims to God, when later they would find Him washing the feet of His disciples, compelling His servitude to those who sought a partnership in His ministry. A bridegroom, Jesus multiplied the joys of good wine to late hours of a wedding, likening the kingdom of heaven to the ten virgins of whom five would be wise to find the spirit to sustain the wait of His return. Promising never to leave or forsake those who come to Him, Jesus' ascension deepened the consolation of the Holy Spirit in those who were convicted by the truth of His life, seeking the everlasting kingdom He often spoke of. By parables about soils, pearls, and talents, Jesus valued the lives of children and adults alike, who found the path to His kingdom in His words to be captivating to the soul. Jesus ordered the raging sea and withered the fig tree when over nature He placed man, delivering Peter from sinking into the water, and cursing the fruitless tree when in due season it didn't yield to His hunger. Out of the rock He promised to raise up sons and daughters, reviving Lazarus after days in the grave, and Tabitha when all thought she was long dead. He fled authorities who sought to crown Him, away from the dwelling of temples made by hands. In His father's house, Jesus claimed, there are many mansions to where He would ascend to prepare for those whom He called. He likened Himself to bread and water in their inseparability from life, promising much more fulfillment than they, that to whomever is given shall never hunger or thirst again. Diligently, Jesus' palms held those who are witnesses to the strength of the nail-driven scars of the cross, to gain all authority that not one of their hairs fall without His knowledge. Worthier than many sparrows, we will soar in the sky to meet Him when He returns, to whom the sting of death had been obliterated. By no greater means has mankind known love than by that of Jesus Christ, who laid down His life that *"whomever believeth in Him shall not perish but have an everlasting life." (John 3:16).*

XXI. Jesus Christ

But who do you say that I Am? (Matthew 16:15)

About the Author

BORN TO A MINISTER, Raed is a third-generation Seventh-Day Adventist, born again Christian. Raed earned his graduate education from Bentley University and George Washington University, where he studied business and engineering, respectively; his undergraduate degree from New York University where he studied information systems. Raed discovered his penmanship during his personal bible study time, heeding to God's revelation in his life after many years outside of the church, where his soul searching expeditions lead him back to the core question about the purpose of life, most profoundly in the story of the cross of Jesus Christ, and His boundless measures in demonstrating God's love, the very purpose that has inspired *In A Mirror.*

Raed believes Jesus Christ's return will bring hope to many who admonish their earthly strife by something more meaningful, attuning to the still voice inside of us, with a much greater capacity than all of our human means. Grateful to the mighty work of God's hands in his life, Raed is thankful to many Christians that have inspired him throughout his life, including his family, his praise and worship ministry teams, and the many others whose lives have brought this book into fruition. It is Raed's aspiration that the words of this book would be a source of blessings and hope to its readers, and a beginning of more testimonies about the power of the word of God and the salvation of Jesus Christ.

Index of Bible Verses

"For every house is built by someone, but God is the builder of everything."
(Hebrews 3:4), p. 7

"For You have delivered my soul from death, have you not kept my feet from falling, that I may walk before God in the light of the living?"
(Psalms 56:13), p. 13

"Blessed be the God and Father of our Lord Jesus Christ, who has blessed us with every blessing in the heavenly places in Christ, just as He chose us in Him before the foundation of the world, that we should be holy and without blame in Him, in love, having predestined us to adoption as sons by Jesus Christ to Himself, according to the good pleasure of His will."
(Ephesians 1:3-5), p. 15

"He who has My commandments and keeps them, it is he who loves Me. And he who loves Me will be loved by My Father, and I will love Him and manifest Myself to him."
(John 14:21), p. 21

"The fear of the Lord is the beginning of wisdom."
(Proverb 9:10), p. 26

"For idols speak delusion, the diviners envision lies, and tell false dreams; they comfort in vain. Therefore, the people wend

their way like sheep; they are in trouble because there is no shepherd."
(Zechariah 10:2), p. 32

"Because of this he is required as for the people, so also for himself, to offer sacrifices for sins. And no man can take this offer to himself, but he who is called by God, just as Aaron was."
(Hebrews 5:3-4), p. 36

"Not by works of righteousness which we have done, but according to His Mercy He saved us through the washing of regeneration and renewing of the Holy Spirit, whom He poured out on us abundantly through Jesus Christ our Savior, that having been justified by His grace we should become heirs according to the hope of eternal life."
(Titus 3:5 – 7), p. 42

"O Death where is your sting? O Hades where is thy victory?"
(1 Corinthians 15:55), p. 47

"I know that my Savior lives, and at the end He will stand on this earth. My flesh may be destroyed, yet from this body I will see God."
(Job 19:25-26), p. 52

"Serve the Lord with fear and rejoice with trembling. Kiss the son, lest He be angry, and you perish in the way, when His wrath in kindled but a little. Blessed are all those who put their trust in Him."
(Psalm 2:11-12), p.56

"Therefore I say to you whatever things you ask when you pray, believe that you receive them, and you will have them."
(Mark 11:24), p. 60

"I charge you O daughter of Jerusalem, by the gazelles or by the deer of the field, do not stir up nor awaken love until it pleases."
(Song of Solomon 2:7), p. 68

"Knowing that a man is not justified by the works of the law, but by faith in Jesus Christ, even we have believed in Christ Jesus, that we might be justified by faith. In Christ and not by the works of the law, for by the works of the law no flesh shall be justified."
(Galatians 2:16), p. 70

"I have no greater joy than to hear that my children walk in truth."
(3 John 1:4), p. 75

"That the sharing of your faith may become effective by the acknowledgement of every good thing which is in you in Christ Jesus."
(Philemon 1:6), p. 79

"My brethren, count it all joy when you fall into various trials, knowing that the testing of your faith produces patience."
(James 1:2), p. 83

"Judge not, and you shall not be judged. Condemn not, and you shall not be condemned. Forgive, and you will be forgiven. Give and it will be given to you: good measure, pressed down, shaken together, and running over will be put in your bosoms. For with the same measure you use, it will be measured back to you."
(Luke 6:37-38), p. 87

"But the hour is coming, and is now here, when the true worshipers will worship the Father in spirit and truth, for the Father is seeking such people to worship him. God is spirit, and those who worship Him must worship in spirit and truth."
(John 4:23-24), p. 92

"I am the Alpha and the Omega, the beginning and the End," says the Lord, "who is and who was and who is to come, the Almighty."
(Revelation 1:8), p. 96

"And Jesus came and spoke unto them, saying, 'All power is given unto me in heaven and in earth.'"
(Matthew 28:18), p. 101